Strength & Dignity

A Proverbs 31 Bible
Study for Young Women

Strength & Dignity: A Proverbs 31 Bible Study for Young Women

kelsey@withstrengthanddignity.com

Copyright © 2020 by Kelsey Pryor.

ISBN 978-1-7345652-0-1

Published by Kelsey Pryor

withstrengthanddignity.com

Dedication

To my three sisters Sydney, Elisa and Kaira. To be raised with such inspirational, talented, joyful, exciting, silly and loving sisters as you has been a blessing indeed.

May we be strong and dignified followers of Christ for the rest of our lives.

Table of Contents

Foreword

by Chelsea Hurst

I am so elated to find you here in the pages of this book. *You* are going to be challenged and encouraged all in one study. Hey, hi. My name is Chelsea Hurst, and I am an author. I love writing and reminding other women who they are in Jesus. Before we get too deep into how excited I am for you, I want to share a little story.

Over the past year, I had been praying for an older mentor (woman) to show up in my life and walk through *all the things* with me. One morning, it was really heavy on my heart that I didn't have an older, godly woman in my life. I began crying (maybe it was that time of the month, lol) and asked God to provide a mentor. I was headed to Panera and started reading the book I sought to read there. It was a Tim Keller book about marriage. I was going to get married in a few months and was seeking all the wisdom and advice I could get! An older gentleman asked me what I was reading, and we began to have a conversation about church, what God has been showing him, and more! He then told me his wife was looking for some younger women to mentor and I was so shocked! At that moment, I was reminded of the kindness of God. He was intentional with me that morning and this man's wife and I have been meeting every week for a while now. Why do I tell you this? Well, I believe when we stand tall and declare the promises and truths that God has given us, then he answers and shows himself in unique ways!

Just like my mentor has taught me how to be a Proverbs 31 woman, these ladies have done the same for you. Full of grace and wisdom, each of them speaks to the characteristics in a profound way. We are going to learn so much together! I'm not sure how you got this study in your hands but let me tell you: you've made no mistake. When we take the time as the busy women that we are, to sit at the Father's feet, He speaks. Not only does He speak to us, but He gives comfort and joy (that's biblical). I'm not sure if you've ever gone a period of time without hanging out with Jesus and then slowly feel yourself becoming snappier, less present, and more selfish... Just me? Okay, hopefully not. BUT! This study is going to show you exactly how to be a purpose-driven woman of the Word. Above all else, we must understand that Proverbs 31 is not a checklist of attributes designed to make women feel inadequate. Instead, it is the opposite! It gives us a glimpse into what it means to be a Christian woman today and the beautiful bride of Christ, His church. With each chapter, we will learn how to take what God says about us all as women and let it be!

We can be told all day who we are, but until we sit and let truth shower over us – it doesn't "stick" with us. In these pages, you will find specific words and calls for us as women to take and run with. The beautiful thing is that we all play such a significant role in the kingdom of God. It is of vital importance that we know our roles! Proverbs 31 isn't a passage that applies to ONLY women who are wives or mothers. It is a call to all women to walk in their specific calling.

I am so excited for you to hear convicting truth, empowering stories, and practical ways to live this out on your own. I believe in you, and I believe in us as women because the God who created us made no mistake. Through each chapter, you will hear the perspective of different women who have all faced unique challenges and were raised in many varying circumstances. Each of them emphasizes on quality traits of a Proverbs 31 woman and urges us to think deeper about the passage itself. Whether you are reading this with a friend, group, or yourself. I was encouraged while going through this study, and I KNOW you will be too. It is an honor to introduce these women and get you excited to embark on the journey ahead! Now let's get started!

Introduction

(read me)

To access the leader guide and companion videos that comes with this book, please email kelsey@withstrengthanddignity.com with your proof of purchase!

Out of all the books you could have picked off the shelf, thanks for picking this one! For perhaps the extent of the chapter's lifetime, Proverbs 31 has been a pathway to Christian wives and mothers. It's a lamp to the footsteps of those who strive to live their lives and lead their households in a way that pleases God.

But what I realized is that it is mainly targeted at wives, and most of the resources out there regarding Proverbs 31 are for wives as well. What about us single girls? It's equally as important for us to study this scripture because it portrays an example of a steadfast, God-fearing woman, but also because most of us *want* to be someone's wife someday.

I'm a firm advocate for challenging one's self, refining one's character and preparation for not only being a mother and wife but also "reigning and ruling" as mandated in Genesis. There are several ways Proverbs 31 could prepare us for motherhood and wifehood but first, here are a few things I thought I'd mention:

- ○ Not all of us will get married! And most of us that will eventually get married will be completely unaware of the timing. It could be within the year or in another ten years! A dangerous thing about preparing for marriage before the appointed time is that we can set our hope on it. So instead of purely looking at this chapter for wives and mothers or potential wives and mothers, I want to use this book to refine ourselves for the sake of looking like Jesus and the godly women God has called us to be! That is just as important and possible to do, regardless of your relationship status.

- ○ The woman you see described in Proverbs 31 is an ideal combination of multiple characteristics and giftings. I doubt you will ever find one single woman who will embody every single characteristic with consistency and perfection, as this chapter describes. We are imperfect humans, and all have different giftings. God does not expect us to be like her all the time. But He does expect us to be constantly searching for ways we can grow, learn, change and be more like Jesus. So, while we will inevitably fall short, holding fast to this example is a good way to challenge yourself.

- Challenge yourself... but *do not beat yourself up*. As stated previously, you will fall short, and that's why we can thank God every day for His gift of grace and redemption through Jesus. We must always strive to be better, but it is worthy to note that we will never attain perfection until we dwell with God.

- Proverbs 31 is scripture. If any of these verses or characteristics explained in this book rubs you the wrong way, don't run away. Simply take a step back and ask yourself why it's rubbing you the wrong way and how you can adjust your thinking to accept it as God's truth, and not simply an opinion. Also, pray about it!

- Don't do this alone. This book is designed for you to do with a Bible study group, friend, or mentor, and I think you'll get more out of it that way.

- Don't be in a hurry.

- Ask questions.

- Take the verses we will give you within the chapters and read the entire context in your own Bible.

- Each of these chapters will be about a Proverbs 31 characteristic or identity. In this context, I've decided to target more values rather than vehicles. We all drive different cars, right? The point isn't which vehicle we take but the road we take to get to our destination. When the passage talks about the woman collecting flax in Proverbs 31, I'm not going to tell you to collect flax. Rather I will tell you to be a hard worker! Your version of hard work and how you see it might look different from someone else's version of working hard, but the point is that we are both working hard.

- **You will need a journal!** We decided to give you writing prompts to help process the content however we didn't want to limit you by giving you lines to write in so please have a journal handy to interact with and answer the prompts!

I also want to let you know why the chapters are laid out, how they are, and how you can go about studying them to get the most out of them.

Again, make sure you use a journal so you can respond to the prompts and process the content better!

- 7 amazing ladies all worked together to write this book, and so we hope you get a lot out of their different stories, backgrounds, opinions and writing styles to help you understand this passage better.

- Each chapter focuses on a characteristic or identity found in Proverbs 31, which emphasizes on the fact that you don't have to be a wife or mother to live it out. Start learning and doing today! Don't wait until you have a ring on that finger.

- The characteristic chapters will be a bit more practical, and the identity chapters might be a bit more thought-provoking or paradigm-shifting. Sometimes the biggest change needs to happen with your beliefs, rather than your actions. What's crazy is, you might not even realize what you are subconsciously believing. We're going to bring some of those things to the surface, propose questions, and give Bible verses to back it up, but the rest of it is up to you to decide on which path to take.

- Each chapter starts with a "God Truth," which answers the question, "What do I need to believe about God in order to embody this characteristic?" For example, "I need to believe that God is great in order for me to be wise and God-fearing."

- Some chapters have personal stories, while some don't. That was up to the author who wrote it. But we find that having a story or example to relate to is often very impactful.

- Each chapter has an application section to help you apply the God Truth and characteristics to your life. Take it seriously and really think outside the box on how you can start making changes in your life.

I could not have written this resource alone, so I combined the stories and wisdom of other women in the making of this book, and you can read all about them in the Author's section at the back of the book. I suggest you give it a look.

Alright, enough chit-chat! Onto the good stuff.

Kelsey

Proverbs

31:10-31

10

A wife of noble character who can find?

She is worth far more than rubies.

11

Her husband has full confidence in her and lacks nothing of value.

12

She brings him good, not harm, all the days of her life.

13

She selects wool and flax and works with eager hands.

14

She is like the merchant ships, bringing her food from afar.

15

She gets up while it is still night; she provides food for her family and portions for her female servants.

16

She considers a field and buys it; out of her earnings she plants a vineyard.

17

She sets about her work vigorously; her arms are strong for her tasks.

18

She sees that her trading is profitable, and her lamp does not go out at night.

19

In her hand she holds the distaff and grasps the spindle with her fingers.

20

She opens her arms to the poor and extends her hands to the needy.

22

She makes coverings for her bed; she is clothed in fine linen and purple.

21

When it snows, she has no fear for her household; for all of them are clothed in scarlet.

23

Her husband is respected at the city gate, where he takes his seat among the elders of the land.

24

She makes linen garments and sells them, and supplies the merchants with sashes.

25

She is clothed with strength and dignity; she can laugh at the days to come.

26

She speaks with wisdom, and faithful instruction is on her tongue.

27

She watches over the affairs of her household and does not eat the bread of idleness.

28

Her children arise and call her blessed; her husband also, and he praises her.

29

"Many women do noble things, but you surpass them all."

30

Charm is deceptive, and beauty is fleeting; but a woman who fears the Lord is to be praised.

31

Honor her for all that her hands have done, and let her works bring her praise at the city gate.

The Gospel

By Kelsey Pryor

I feel it is necessary to preface these next 10 chapters with a clear message so that all who read this book should proclaim it as the truth. We can all vary in our beliefs about lifestyle, politics, menial or complicated theological topics, and the interpretation of certain verses in the Bible. But if you are reading this book, either alone or in a group, I felt it would be helpful to lay out the foundation on which we should be building our faith. Even if you're a professing Christian, it never hurts to remind yourself of these truths.

So here it is.

Truth 1

"In the beginning, God created the heavens and the earth."

-Genesis 1:1

Open your Bible to Genesis 1-2 and read about how the earth and everything in it came to be just by the word of the Lord and the perfection with which it was all set in motion. You will also discover how God's desire when He created the earth and set it in motion was to walk in the cool of the day with us! He wanted to know us intimately, and through the perfection of all individuals, there existed unity between Him and His creation. There existed only one rule: not to eat the fruit off of a certain tree in the garden. By doing this, we would show our loyalty, love and trust in Him.

Truth 2

"So when the woman saw that the tree was good for food, and that it was a delight to the eyes, and that the tree was to be desired to make one wise, she took of its fruit and ate, and she also gave some to her husband who was with her, and he ate. Then the eyes of both were opened, and they knew that they were naked. And they sewed fig leaves together and made themselves loincloths."

–Genesis 3:6-7

Read Genesis 3 to learn about the fall of mankind. The Lord's will was for us to live in unity with Him walking in a beautiful garden which He created perfectly. But when Adam and Eve ate the forbidden fruit, it led to the separation between us and the Almighty. What is perfect (God) cannot be in union with what is not perfect (us). The clean cannot be with the unclean.

Truth 3

The law was created in order to teach people how to live and atone for their sins in an attempt to correct our transgressions. There are actually over 600 laws in the Old Covenant, but here are the predominant 10:

"You shall have no other gods before me. You shall not make for yourself a carved image, or any likeness of anything that is in heaven above, or that is in the earth beneath, or that is in the water under the earth. You shall not bow down to them or serve them, for I the LORD your God am a jealous God, visiting the iniquity of the fathers on the children to the third and the fourth generation of those who hate me, but showing steadfast love to thousands of those who love me and keep my commandments. You shall not take the name of the LORD your God in vain, for the LORD will not hold him guiltless who takes his name in vain. Remember the Sabbath day, to keep it holy. Six days you shall labor, and do all your work, but the seventh day is a Sabbath to the LORD your God. On it you shall not do any work, you, or your son, or your daughter, your male servant, or your female servant, or your livestock, or the sojourner who is within your gates. For in six days the LORD made heaven and earth, the sea, and all that is in them, and rested on the seventh day. Therefore the LORD blessed the Sabbath day and made it holy. Honor your father and your mother, that your days may be long in the land that the LORD your God is giving you. You shall not murder. You shall not commit adultery. You shall not steal. You shall not bear false witness against your neighbor. You shall not covet your neighbor's house; you shall not covet your neighbor's wife, or his male servant, or his female servant, or his ox, or his donkey, or anything that is your neighbor's."

-Exodus 20:3-17

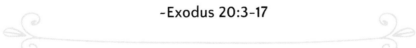

It's easy for us to say we have kept the law because the ones we remember are "do not kill, do not steal, do not worship idols." But have you ever lied, disrespected your parents, become jealous of someone, lusted after anyone, or valued an object over your relationship with and the will of God? Then guess what? You're a sinner. And so am I! We are guilty just as Adam and Eve were guilty when they sinned in the garden.

Truth 4

"For the wages of sin is death..."

-Romans 6:23

We deserve to die for our sins. God is a just God and must hold someone accountable for sin. The price that we must pay for transgressing against God is our lives, and as sinners, hell awaits those who aren't in communion with Him, which is eternal separation from God.

Truth 5

God is also a loving Father, and He found another way. Did you know the full verse that I quoted above?

"For the wages of sin is death, but the free gift of
God is eternal life in Christ Jesus our Lord."

-Romans 6:23

The triune God sent down his only Son, Jesus Christ, to earth as a normal human to live a normal but perfect life so He could ultimately fulfill the prophecies of old by dying on the cross. Thus, perfection was traded for imperfection. Taking our place in judgment, Jesus has willingly given us the gift of union with God by taking the place of those willing to accept His gift.

"But he was pierced for our transgressions, he was crushed for our iniquities;
the punishment that brought us peace was on him,
and by his wounds we are healed."

-Isaiah 53:5

God then raised Jesus from the dead when He ascended into Heaven to be with His Father until the unknown appointed time when He will return and judge the world in righteousness.

Truth 6

This gift is available to you! On the day on which your soul will be judged, God will judge you to be sinful, thus worthy of eternal separation from Him. UNLESS you:

"[C]onfess with your mouth that Jesus is Lord and believe in your heart that God raised him from the dead, you will be saved."

-Romans 10:9

In this case, Jesus will say, "God, I have switched places with them. My perfect record is now theirs, and I will take on their sinful record as my own." This is a gift from Jesus that is free for you to accept or reject. But be warned that if you reject this gift, your sentence on judgement day will be eternal separation from God, or as the Bible calls it, Hell.

Action item: Have you accepted Jesus as Lord of your life and Savior over your soul? If not, you can do this very simply on your own by telling Jesus that He is Lord over your life and repenting from your life of sin and giving Him your life to use to advance His will and Kingdom on earth. If you feel like you need help and instruction, you can either start this conversation with your Bible Study leader, Christian parents, trusted people at Church, or contact us, the Strength and Dignity team, at withstrengthanddignity.com. We would be happy to talk to you about Jesus, how to make Him Lord of your life, and what that looks like!

If you have decided to give Jesus Lordship over your life, this is a HUGE step. It might be simple, but it is life-changing, and so your life must change as well. Paul makes it very clear that under the sacrifice of Jesus, we no longer have to live by the law to be saved. But if our hearts truly desire Jesus to be Lord, then we must make every effort to die to our fleshly desires and live more like Jesus would in truth, love and righteousness. Knowing we will fall short because of our sinful nature and that the blood of Jesus will atone for our sins does not give us a "get out of jail free" card to just do whatever the heck we want!

"What shall we say then? Are we to continue in sin that grace may abound?
By no means! How can we who died to sin still live in it? Do you not know that
all of us who have been baptized into Christ Jesus were baptized into his death?
We were buried therefore with him by baptism into death, in order that,
just as Christ was raised from the dead by the glory of the Father,
we too might walk in newness of life."

-Romans 6:1-4

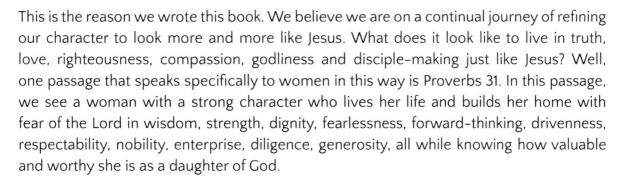

This is the reason we wrote this book. We believe we are on a continual journey of refining our character to look more and more like Jesus. What does it look like to live in truth, love, righteousness, compassion, godliness and disciple-making just like Jesus? Well, one passage that speaks specifically to women in this way is Proverbs 31. In this passage, we see a woman with a strong character who lives her life and builds her home with fear of the Lord in wisdom, strength, dignity, fearlessness, forward-thinking, drivenness, respectability, nobility, enterprise, diligence, generosity, all while knowing how valuable and worthy she is as a daughter of God.

So, that's what we want to dive into now. How can we refine our character to more accurately represent Christ? We are perfectly imperfect, daughters of the King and resolutely feminine. Let's start acting like it.

Wise & God-Fearing

By Addie Parris

Proverbs 31:26, 30

She speaks with wisdom, and faithful instruction is on her tongue.
Charm is deceptive and beauty is fleeting; but a woman
who fears the Lord is to be praised.

Wisdom (n) 1. the quality of having experience, knowledge, and good judgment; the quality of being wise. 2. the soundness of an action or decision with regard to the application of experience, knowledge, and good judgment.

God-fearing (adj) 1. having a reverent feeling toward God: Devout.

God is Great

If we're honest with ourselves, we know that emulating the life of the Proverbs 31 woman is an intimidating and impossible task. So, as a precursor, let me try to encourage you by saying that it's *okay* to not be perfect at all or in any of the qualities we talk about in this study. However, we've structured this study in a strategic and specific way. It was no coincidence that "Wise and God-fearing" is the first of the characteristics we wanted to look at. Why? This characteristic is a common thread among all the women we are going to study in the Bible. And just like you and I, they weren't perfect either.

Sarah mocked God when He told her she was going to have a child and had little faith in Him. Rahab was a prostitute. Ruth was an idol worshiper.

These women had their fair share of flaws, but what was remarkable about them is the fact that they had wisdom and feared the Lord. Through this, Sarah became the mother of the Jewish nation. Rahab helped the Israelites (God's chosen people) by betraying her own people. Ruth left everything she knew to help her Mother-in-Law and became an ancestor to Christ. These women, even in their faults, were able to do amazing things for the Kingdom, but it was all through wisdom and fear of the Lord.

The word "wisdom" is mentioned 218 times throughout the Bible, more than the scriptures talk about grace, joy, and praying. We're also told wisdom is better than *gold* (Proverbs 15:33). By knowing these two things, we can immediately see there is an importance to the word. For many, however, this term can be somewhat confusing. What does wisdom mean, and how can anything be better than something as rare and as highly regarded as gold?

A phrase we also see mentioned a lot in the Bible is "fear of the Lord." Each time we come across this phrase, what comes to mind is, how do I fear God? Am I supposed to be *scared* of God? Again, what does that even mean?

Despite our confusion, these two ideas are mentioned over and over again in scripture. And if we dive deeper into the Word, we will see that somehow, they are connected.

"The fear of the Lord is the beginning of wisdom."

-Proverbs 9:10

Rewrite this verse.

*TIP: use a journal to complete all prompts and questions throughout the book.

"The fear of the LORD is instruction in wisdom, and humility comes before honor.."

-Proverbs 15:33

So, let's flesh out the questions: what is wisdom? What does it mean to fear the Lord? And why is it wise to fear our Creator? Before continuing, write your current answer to these questions!

Wisdom and fear of the Lord are essential to life as followers of Jesus. But before we can see the true value of having those qualities, we must first understand some things about God.

The New Testament does such a great job of demonstrating the Father's love for His creation. We see that God's love for us is deep, high, and wide (Ephesians 3:18). He says that He will leave everything to come and find us when we go astray (Matthew 18:22), and we are told that nothing can separate us from His love (Romans 8:39).

We also see God's greatest demonstration of love for us through the cross.

"For God so loved the world, that he gave his only Son, that whoever believes in him should not perish but have eternal life."

- John 3:16

God's love and adoration for us is oozing out of the pages of our bibles. But if you've ever spent any time reading in the Old Testament, it almost seems as if God had a personality transplant.

In Genesis, God said that the whole world was corrupt. Therefore, He flooded the earth and killed every human being except Noah and his family. In Exodus, God inflicted 10 plagues on the people of Egypt, which included boils all over their bodies, locusts, and the death of every firstborn son. In Joshua, God *hurled* hailstones down on a people group and killed them.

Yikes.

This is a stark contrast from the loving and compassionate God we see in the New Testament. Yet, the scriptures say that God does not change (Malachi 3:6). Therefore, God is just as gentle and tender in the Old Testament as He is in the New Testament. Also, He is as just and wrathful in the New Testament as he was in the Old Testament.

God is the one who tells the lightning where to strike (Job 36:32) and His thoughts outnumber the grains of sand (Psalm 139:18). He spoke life into existence (Genesis 1).

God designed the 332,519,000 cubic miles of water on the planet. He handcrafted the Himalayas, Rockies, and Andes. He single-handedly created 950,000 species of insects.

That same God knows even the smallest and most intricate details of who you are, like the exact number of hairs on your head (Luke 12:7). He knows when you sit and when you stand back up (Psalm 139:2). God is all-knowing and all-powerful.

His identities are many. He is Father, Creator, Protector, and Savior.

He is the Creator of all things. He is not dependent on anything or anyone. He's present and active, deeply invested in our lives, and sovereign over all things; He always has been and always will be. He is all that we need Him to be and more.

In Exodus, God said to Moses, "you cannot see my face, for no one may see me and live" (Exodus 33:20). God is so great that if we get to see His face, we would not survive. It's hard to even fathom that, but it is true.

His power is immeasurable. His beauty is incomprehensible. His knowledge is inconceivable.

He is omnipresent, which means He's everywhere present at the same time. He is omniscient, which means He knows everything. God is omnipotent, which means He is all-powerful. God did not have to learn anything and never will. Nothing is hidden or unknown to Him. He can do whatever He wants and whenever He wants. He does not run out of energy or resources.

It is imperative that we get to a place in our walk with Jesus, where we stand in awe of God and attempt to understand his greatness. While we will never be able to grasp exactly how big Yahweh is, we need to realize how small we are in comparison.

> *"Great is our Lord, and abundant in power; his understanding is beyond measure."*
>
> - Psalm 147:5

A.W. Tozer once wrote, "What comes to our mind when we think about God is the most important thing about us." Deep down, who do you see God as? Do you see Him as a powerful, loving, gracious, and just God? Or do you see Him as a distant, indifferent, uninterested, cold, and judgemental God? More often than not, we have a small view of who God really is. However, if we have a small idea of who God is, we will never see the need to fear Him or desire the wisdom to be like Him.

It is only when we have some sort of understanding of the greatness of God will we see our desperate need for wisdom. Only then will we be able to fear the Lord. To fear the Lord, we must admit to our insignificance and lack of control. We must always humble ourselves before Him at all times.

> *"He must become greater; I must become less"*
>
> - John 3:30

Rewrite this verse. How does it make you feel?

When we fear the Lord, we will want to follow His ways. We will want to do what He tells us and keep the commands He gives us. When we fear Him, we would be afraid of what would happen if we stray away.

I love the way John Piper explains it. He says, "I think fearing God means that God is in your mind and heart. He is so powerful, so holy, and so awesome that you would not *dare* to run away from Him but only run *to* him. " God knows what's best and wants good things for us. In His presence we have fullness of joy (Psalm 16:11). The scriptures say, "No eye has seen, no ear has heard, no mind has conceived what God has prepared for those who love him" (Isaiah 64:4). Why would we ever want to leave a God like that?

Piper continues, saying, "Tremble if you ever feel any inclination to leave this God. There is only destruction away from Him."

Let's read that again: "There is *only destruction* away from Him."

. . . .

"The thief comes only to steal and kill, and destroy; I have come that they may have life, and have it to the full"

- John 10:10

We should not dare to run away from God because of who is after us; the "thief" or Satan, our enemy. Don't take the words "steal, kill, and destroy" lightly. There is a real spiritual battle happening right now. Proverbs 19:23 encaptures this concept well, "The fear of the Lord leads to life: then one rests content, untouched by trouble." The Lord is our protector, strength, and shield. But when we stay away from Him, the scriptures make it clear that we will face trouble.

Meditate on the importance of clinging to God. Do you fully believe that it is in your best interest to remain by his side? Why? Do you agree that the fear of the Lord is the only way to do so? Why?

So, how do we cling to God? How do we discern His ways?

This is where wisdom comes in.

To start, let's clear up a common misconception about what wisdom is. Wisdom is not *only* a bunch of facts or knowledge. It's not being able to spout off all the verses you have memorized or facts about the Bible.

The Apostle Paul makes this point clear in his letter to the Corinthians:

. . . .

"We know that "We all possess knowledge." But knowledge puffs up while love builds up."

- 1 Corinthians 8:1

Knowledge has its place, and the book of Proverbs has a lot of positive things to say about it. However, it does stress that it can lead to pride.

You've probably heard of the common phrase "knowledge is power," but I beg to differ. If we have a lot of knowledge but choose not to act on it or do anything with it, it means nothing.

Wisdom is putting knowledge into practice. It is because of this truth that wisdom is power.

The Bible talks about wisdom often. In fact, the purpose of the book of Proverbs is to help us attain wisdom and discipline (Proverbs 1:2).

Let's look at what Proverbs 3 has to say about wisdom:

"Blessed is the one who finds wisdom, and the one who gets understanding, for the gain from her is better than gain from silver and her profit better than gold. She is more precious than jewels, and nothing you desire can compare with her. Long life is in her right hand; in her left hand are riches and honor. Her ways are ways of pleasantness, and all her paths are peace. She is a tree of life to those who lay hold of her; those who hold her fast are called blessed."

- Proverbs 3:13-18

As this verse shows us, we gain much through wisdom. God wants to bless us in ways we can hardly imagine when we take hold of the knowledge we are given through the scripture and prayer so we can apply it to our lives. We gain a *large* profit when we consciously choose to embrace the understanding we are given.

Recap this section in your own words. How can the truth of "God is Great" help us become wise and God-fearing?

Personal Story

Going into my freshman year of high school, I already felt I was at a crossroads about what type of person I wanted to be. I wasn't following Jesus yet, but unbeknownst to me, God had and was planting seeds in my heart. However, even before my first day of high school, I was already getting attention from upperclassmen guys and getting sucked into the lure of popularity. As my freshman year went on, I started dating a guy that I had been crushing on for months. I was convinced that life could not get any better.

Then, the summer after my freshman year, I encountered Jesus in a way I never had before. I had no idea what giving my life to Christ looked like, but I knew I wanted the life He offered to the fullest (John 10:10).

After that, my life began to look different. I began reading my Bible, my friendships were becoming deeper, and I started to learn what it looked like to be a follower of Christ. However, as I grew in my relationship with Jesus, I began to have an internal conflict about whether I should continue to date my boyfriend or not.

In the eyes of the world, our relationship looked great. He was kind, funny, handsome, his family loved me, and mine loved him too. We were both well-liked at school and played on multiple sports teams. But there was one big issue. We were in completely different spots in our relationship with God.

I was all in for Jesus, but I was being held back by the relationship I was in. We weren't on the same page and we weren't fighting on the same team. I was in the business of telling my friends about Jesus while he was in the business of winning the next football game. After beginning to follow Jesus, I wanted to date for marriage. I didn't want to date just any guy I thought was cute or one that would give me attention.

The scriptures say that I am a daughter of the King, God's dwelling place, royalty, chosen and loved. I wanted to be with someone who would see me and treat me in the same way God sees me and treats me. I knew that if the guy I was dating was not following Jesus, he would never see me that way.

I knew what needed to be done. We needed to break up, but I didn't want to. He said he loved me. He told me I was beautiful. I got the attention I so desperately desired but the satisfaction from that was momentary.

But if we broke up, what would my boyfriend think of me? Surely, he wouldn't understand. What would people around me think when they found out I broke up with him for Jesus? Surely,

I would be made fun of.

Yet, I felt the Lord telling me to trust Him and that He had something better for me. I knew that if I continued to date my boyfriend, I would miss out on how God wanted to use me. And I knew that by continuing to date him, I could be missing out on the man God had for me to marry, and how he wanted to prepare my heart for him. I also knew that if I continued to date him, I would be deliberately going against what God was asking of me. I would be sinning against God.

As I thought about all of this, 1 Corinthians 2:9d stuck out to me,

"But, as it is written, "What no eye has seen, nor ear heard, nor the heart of man imagined, what God has prepared for those who love him."

I realized that God's plans for me were far better than anything I could think of. I could have a *good* life with the plans *I* had made for myself, or I could step out in faith and walk into the *great* plans *God* had for my life.

It was through fear of the Lord and wisdom that I decided to break up with my boyfriend. At the time, it was hard and painful. We dated for nearly three years. But I had the God-given wisdom to know that our relationship was not glorifying Jesus and was not pushing me toward the feet of Him. The scriptures say, "let us throw off everything that hinders and the sin that so easily entangles" (Hebrews 12:1). My relationship was hindering me from doing what God had for me and was constantly entangling me in sin.

I also had enough fear of the Lord to know that if I continued to date him, I would be disobedient to what God was asking of my life. I would grow further apart from God, and I would fall into sin. I was scared to miss out on the amazing plans God had for me, and to drift away from Him. In Hebrews Chapter 10:26-27 says, if we deliberately keep on sinning after we have received the knowledge of the truth, no sacrifice for sins is left, but only the fearful expectation of judgement. I knew that by continuing to date my boyfriend, I would be deliberately sinning and have to face the judgement of God.

Can you think of a time you have related to this story? Journal about how the fear of the Lord could have or did affect your situation. Are you still in a situation like Addie? Consider giving that over to the Lord and seeing what He wants you to do.

Application

So, how do we find wisdom?

Perhaps, the easiest way of getting this is just by asking.

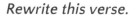

"If any of you lacks wisdom, you should ask God, who gives generously to all without finding fault, and it will be given to you."

— James 1:5

Rewrite this verse.

Simple enough, right? God wants to give good things to His children!

Another way of gaining wisdom is through our day-to-day life.

As humans, one of the best tools we have for learning is experience. Someone who wants to be a chef can read as many books as they want on cooking, but nothing compares to putting a knife to the cutting board and physically doing it yourself.

That's why wisdom is putting our knowledge into practice. It simply means taking the commands God gives us in the Bible and applying them in our daily lives. It's studying the scriptures and observing where and how we see God at work. It's taking the words that are said in the Bible and seeing how Jesus acted and applying them to situations we come across.

"Who is wise and understanding among you? Let them show it by their good life, by deeds done in the humility that comes from wisdom."

— James 3:13

Wisdom is also directly connected with humility. In order to gain wisdom, we must realize that we are not as mature and knowledgeable as we think we are. In Jeremiah 17:9, it says, "the heart is deceitful above all things and beyond cure. Who can understand it?"

Our hearts are deceitful. We have false motives, selfish desires, and we tend to mess up. Oftentimes, this happens without us even realizing it! We are imperfect humans in an imperfect world. Yes, through Jesus, we are seen as perfect but that doesn't mean that every decision we make is perfect. That's why we're told to work out our salvation with fear and trembling (Philippians 2:12). We must be humble enough to admit that sometimes we just get it wrong.

One of the wisest things for us to do as young followers of Jesus is to seek wise counsel. This can be done through daily reading of the Word, which are the *actual* words of God... I mean, what better source of wisdom? And also seeking wisdom from more mature and trusted believers around us. This is reiterated many times throughout Proverbs.

"The way of a fool is right in his own eyes, but a wise man listens to advice."

– Proverbs 12:15

Rewrite this verse.

"Listen to advice and accept instruction, that you may gain wisdom in the future. Many are the plans in the mind of a man, but it is the purpose of the Lord that will stand."

— Proverbs 19:20-21

"For by wise guidance you can wage your war, and in abundance of counselors there is victory."

— Proverbs 24:6

Friends, it is vital that we invite older and wiser people into our lives and into our decision making. Oftentimes, they catch mistakes or areas of trouble we are unable to spot. They've been through our season of life before and can speak from experience of what they've learned since then or what they wish they knew during that time.

However, we have to be humble enough to ask for others' thoughts and opinions, to admit that we don't know everything, and sometimes to hear what we might not *want* to hear at the moment. Humility is the key to obtaining wisdom.

This is the same with fear of the Lord. Without humility, we will never see the need to submit to His greatness and power.

God doesn't tell us to fear Him and desire wisdom so He can control us or get us to do whatever He wants. He's not a dictator. He gives us a choice to be obedient and to follow Him. But He tells us to fear Him and seek wisdom because it leads to our joy, success, and a vibrant and intimate relationship with Him during our lives on earth.

Don't forget how much He loves and cares for you. He *wants* us to be happy, and He *wants* us to have a life of abundance. The way to a life like that is through Him. It's through wisdom and fear of the Lord.

But what about the fear of the Lord? How can we apply that to our lives? Here's the way I like to think about it: Our relationship with God has three motives or reasons which are: love, trust and fear. While all three should be constantly present, sometimes we are driven by one motive more than the others.

Our relationship with God is most healthy when we dwell in the love layer, which is undergirded by trust and fear. We operate out of love for Him and a firm belief in His love for us. Everything we do, say and think is because we just love God so much and know how deeply we are truly loved.

But it's hard to stay in such a constant state of firm love and faith like that, and so, we often slip into the trust motive. We might be struggling with loving God, but we trust Him. We know He is good and righteous, and His will is sovereign and we trust Him in that.

Then when our trust in God wavers, we have fear to catch us. You might have a hard time loving or trusting Him, but you are scared of disappointing Him, of judgement, of being a sinner in His eyes and thus deserving of death. Being afraid of the wrath of God might sound like God has a bit of a problem... "if he loves me, why would He be wrathful?" But we often forget that wrath is actually part of love. Think about if you had a child, and they came home from school completely beaten up and bullied. If you don't get angry, your love for your child could be questionable. But if you are filled with rage that this would happen to your child... that rage is coming out of a deep love. The same is applicable when we do something outside of God's will. He sees the result as destruction, danger and separation from Him and He is filled with a jealous rage for the heart of His child.

I'm reminded of Narnia's "The Lion, the Witch and the Wardrobe," when 4 human children enter C.S. Lewis's fantasy world to discover they are the only ones who can save it. However, in doing so, they must follow the rightful king of the land; the Lion, Aslan, who represents Jesus. As two beavers tell the children about the lion, they inquire, if he was safe.

Mr. Beaver laughs and says, "Of course he isn't safe! But he's good." That phrase is so powerful to me when I think about the ferocious beast ruling Narnia. No one would say a lion is safe! But everyone knows that's exactly why they should follow him and shows them he can win. Yet, he doesn't rule with a cruel viciousness. *He is good.* And that fact alone can still your heart into a firm resolve to realize, "This is someone worthy of following."

· · · · · · · · · · · · · · · · · ·

" 'Why do you call me good?' Jesus answered.
'No one is good – except God alone.' "

- Mark 10:18

Answer these questions:

> *Have you ever wrestled with your fear of the Lord? By which I mean, have you ever asked God to help you fear Him and be in awe of Him even more?*
>
> *Have you ever asked God for more wisdom or to bring wise people into your life?*
>
> *Do you fear God? Do you tremble when you consider sinning or realize you have sinned? Do you have a desire to please Him?*

If your answer to any of the above questions was no, consider praying for those right now.

This is a deep and important issue to struggle and wrestle with because if your answer to any of the above questions was "no," you will have a hard time realizing why the rest of this book even applies to you. If you aren't trying to get closer to God every single day, living a life like Jesus, repenting from wrongdoings, having a teachable spirit in order to refine your heart and character, and having your eyes set on the eternal Kingdom…. Then why would you want to become a woman of God?

> *Have you ever stopped to reflect on the greatness and power of God? Take some time to do so now. You could go for a walk, journal, or do whatever you want. Whatever you do though, slow yourself down. Don't rush through this time.*
>
> *Think of how He spoke things into existence. Consider how He exists outside of time and space. Give thought to how such a big God wants a personal and deep relationship with you.*
>
> *In this time of reflection, ask God for wisdom. Pray for humility. Pray that He would bring you to a place where you stand in awe of Him.*

Group Questions

1. Those who are willing, share your answers to the above questions. Do you recognize the magnitude of your answer to these questions? Did your answer to these questions reveal anything to you about the way you think or live or commune with God?

2. Do you have a regular time in your life when you spend time in the Word? Do you realize the importance of having such a time?

3. Do you have someone in your life that you trust and feel is more mature in their faith than you, and is able to advise and guide you?

4. Discuss other ways you might seek after wisdom wholeheartedly.

Group Blessing

Lord, we stand in awe of your greatness. We thank you for your unfathomable strength, creativity, goodness, justice and love. We understand you are the source of all wisdom and you are the redeemer of humanity. We surrender our will to yours. We ask that you fill us with great fear for your greatness and overwhelm us with your love. Bestow upon us wisdom so we might please you in all that we do and live in a way according to your will.

Amen.

Valuable and Worthy

By Kelsey Pryor

Proverbs 31:10-11

A wife of noble character who can find?
She is worth far more than rubies.
Her husband has full confidence in her and lacks nothing of value.

Valuable *(a) 1. Deserving esteem. 2. A precious possession.*

Worthy *(n) 1. Having worth or excellence; possessing merit; valuable; deserving; estimable; excellent; virtuous.*

God gives us rest

Have you ever wondered where your worth comes from? What makes you valuable? Why are you here on this planet? I think humanity as a whole has struggled for a long time to answer these questions... So, there's really no way that I, a 19-year-old high school graduate sitting here on my bedroom floor, will be able to solve these deep questions that have plagued humanity since the beginning of time. But I can do my best to let you in on my analysis of the situation, i.e., bringing you into the pep talk I give myself when I struggle with this idea (which, believe me, is a whole lot.)

One unique thing about this chapter is that it focuses on identity, not necessarily a characteristic. So, while I'm going to do my best to provide a reason for this identity and application for what we talk about, it really boils down to you personally taking on the identity yourself. *You are valuable. You are worthy.*

Do you believe you are valuable and worthy? Why or why not?

The verse above states that this Proverbs 31 woman is worth far more than rubies. Her husband has full confidence in her, and he lacks nothing of value. This simply means that his marriage to her was quite a valuable thing. That can sound like a lot to live up to. "How can I do that so that my future husband can find his marriage to be a valuable thing? So that he can have full confidence in me? How can I become worth far more than rubies?"

Maybe you think the easiest thing I could do is give you a checklist of exactly how to become this way. (I mean, I love lists, so if that were the case, I'd be pretty happy about it.) But what if I told you it was simultaneously simpler than that, yet so much harder?

You can't become more valuable by doing more. Genesis Chapter 1 says that we were made in the image of God... God, the divine being whose name we are commanded to not even misuse... who called the stars and trees into existence with a single word from His mouth. Yes, *that* God chose to bestow His image inside of you before you were born. Which means before you even did anything worthwhile! You can't give yourself more worth through your accomplishments. Your status, whether you're an international sensation like Taylor Swift or Sally Smith from the deli, will have no effect on your inherent worth.

What do you think the "image of God" is?

You are fearfully and wonderfully knit together with caring hands (Psalm 139) and while you were still a sinner, Jesus Christ and God himself, chose to *sacrifice everything* for you! (Romans 5)

Where do you get your worth from? List a few accomplishments, positions, or achievements that have often been a source of worth for you:

There is an agnostic idea that people are inherently valuable because they are people. That's a strange thing to believe because I think the opposite is easily said by people who think that humans are a cancer to the planet and provide no worth whatsoever and if we stopped existing then the world would be a better place. So that can't be the answer...

So, where does it come from then? If not our humanity...

Now, this is going to sound cheesy or cliché, but I think most things only become cheesy or cliché when they are said over and over again because they are the simplest and most foundational of truths: It comes from God.

Jordan Peterson has some brilliant things to say on this topic. While his religious beliefs are somewhat unknown, I think this great quote is still very relevant. "Regardless of your inadequacies and malevolence, you have a moral obligation to assume that despite all evidence, there is actually something of intrinsic worth about you, and as a consequence, you are duty-bound to treat yourself like that is true."[a] That very thing that gives us our intrinsic worth *is God*.

Write "My value comes from God. He calls me worthy."

I'm going to go in a different direction here for a bit, but I promise I'll tie this all back together in a minute.

Let's talk about rest for a second. The idea of rest is infused into the fabric of the Bible, but we don't always see it or think it's worthy of noting. Of course, the first place we see it is in the account of creation.

"So God blessed the seventh day and made it holy, because on it God rested from all his work that he had done in creation."

- Genesis 2:3

One may begin to wonder, *why did God rest?* Was He tired? God is a being without limitations, so that's not the answer.

Without reading ahead, why do you think God rested?

Jesus gives us the answer in John 19:30 when he says, "It is finished." The work was complete. That's why God rested.

This is important to note before we dive into being valuable and worthy because we must remember that it is not of our own accord that we are valuable and worthy, just like it is not of our own accord that we are able to rest.

Rewrite that last sentence, starting at "it is not..."

We have so much work to do! We could tirelessly pursue what must be justified, but it will not work. There is nothing we can do that will justify our sinful nature. Our checklist will never be complete. We will never be able to do anything that will make us worthy of sacrifice or valuable enough to die for. *But God has decided we are valuable and worthy of His sacrifice through His own love and desires. Not by anything we ourselves have done.*

When we remember that and when we truly believe it, it will cause us to step back and simply worship. One way to worship God is to rest. It shows Him you put everything in His hands and that you trust His ability to hold the world together while you take time to rest in His presence.

Is there anything about resting or taking a day off that scares you?

Take a look at King David, for example. The Psalms are laced with his understanding of the rest that can only come from the Lord:

"I lay down and slept; I woke again, for the LORD sustained me."

-Psalm 3:5

"In peace I will both lie down and sleep; for you alone, O LORD, make me dwell in safety."

-Psalm 4:8

"He makes me lie down in green pastures. He leads me beside still waters. He restores my soul. He leads me in paths of righteousness for his name's sake."

-Psalm 23:2-3

"For God alone my soul waits in silence; from him comes my salvation. He alone is my rock and my salvation, my fortress; I shall not be greatly shaken."

-Psalm 62:1-2

"Return, O my soul, to your rest; for the Lord has dealt bountifully with you."

-Psalm 116:7

Worship the Lord. Thank Him for His ways. Recognize His sacrifice and the magnitude of His worth that is reflected through you, His most beloved creation. Do this through resting. Trusting that *It. Is. Finished.* Your time to work is over because even though you didn't do everything you could have done, He has already done it for you. That is the only way you can rest. And *that* my friend, is where our belief that we are valuable and worthy, should come from.

Recap this section in your own words. How can the truth "God Gives us Rest" help us believe we are valuable and worthy?

Application

Now, assuming we fully believe that we are valuable and worthy, which might take a long time to accomplish, how do you apply that belief to your actions?

I know that I have a hard time not getting my worth from other people. What my parents, friends, and even strangers think of me is an easy place to find my value. (Did I mention guys? Yeah... that plays a big part too.) But it never lasts. *Putting the pressure of the value of your existence on another person is too much for anyone to bear.* One time I made the mistake of telling someone that if they stopped loving me, I would feel worthless. They freaked out and pushed me away which resulted just as I had said it would: I felt worthless. Because I was putting the pressure of the value of my existence on their shoulders and that load was far too heavy.

Lots of people find their worth in their jobs, in their nice house, in their good deeds... the list goes on and on. What's interesting about all those material things is that they can easily be taken away. You could lose your job. Your house could burn down or get flooded, or you might not make enough money to keep it. No matter how many good deeds you accomplish, you are a sinful human who will always mess up eventually.

Referring to the list of things you made before, of things that you draw your worth from, have any of those things or people ever let you down? How?

So how can you start to believe that your value comes not from these things, but from the Lord?

One important step is to bathe yourself in the truth regularly. What are you spending your time reading or watching, and who are you spending your time with? It's important to balance the areas of your life that lack accountability or responsibility with time spent with the Lord, in His Word, and be surrounded by others that love and follow Him.

Is there anything you spend your time doing or anyone you spend your time with that could be allowing lies to seep in, telling you that you aren't valuable?

I don't know about you, but as soon as I'm outside the watchful gaze of people who love and care about me (mainly my parents), it's a lot easier for me to listen to the lies that always start with "you are not enough." This happens at home when I'm around my parents too, but through some of my independent travels, I've found that as soon as I step foot in that airport, the lies come at me 10 times harder. Why is that? I think somehow, I'm letting my guard down. I'm insecure and unsure of myself in unfamiliar surroundings, and the enemy takes advantage of that vulnerable place. Are you often in a situation where you can go long periods of time without truth being spoken over you? Another example is when I got myself my own Netflix account and wanted to watch a murder mystery show. One of the first results was "How to Get Away with Murder." Sounds intriguing, right? Yeah, well, 4 episodes in and I was hooked on the story so much that I easily ignored the debauchery, unwholesome and dark themes I was simultaneously exposing myself to. The few weeks it took me to watch that season I could sense an actual change in my demeanor, attitude, and security in my worth... but I had to finish because it was so "good," right??

Watch yourself girl! The enemy can sneak in ways we don't expect, and one of the biggest things he is after is to destroy your belief that you are valuable and worthy.

. . . .

"Be sober-minded; be watchful. Your adversary the devil prowls around like a roaring lion, seeking someone to devour. Resist him, firm in your faith, knowing that the same kinds of suffering are being experienced by your brotherhood throughout the world. And after you have suffered a little while, the God of all grace, who has called you to his eternal glory in Christ, will himself restore, confirm, strengthen and establish you."

-1 Peter 5:8

Do you think any of those things or people that you listed are worth cutting out or taking a second look at? How might you change that situation so that you aren't letting the enemy and his lies sneak in?

Next, I think it's also important to start telling or showing other people that *they* are valuable. Show them that *they* are worthy. If you start speaking that identity over other people, and you truly believe it, it will become harder to deny that truth for yourself. Meditate on this verse that calls us into our identity and actually shows us the origin of our value and worth in God:

"So God created man in his own image, in the image of God he created him; male and female he created them."

- Genesis 1:27

Rewrite this verse in your own words:

Why is being an "image bearer" important? First, it's unique to humans. No other part of creation bears the Kings Insignia like we do. This is not only reflected by our physical appearance but also through our souls, our creativity, our ideas, delight and ability to worship. At one point in his life, C.S. Lewis was struck by this phenomenon and wondered what life would be like if we treated everyone like we should; as people bearing the image of the Lord Almighty. One way he did this was to respond to every single letter sent to him. As his fame grew, he received quite a few letters a day... *and he responded to every single one.* He treated everyone like the human with a soul and the image bearer they were. He realized that they all have stories, heartaches, ideas, desires, joys, sorrows... but most importantly, they bore the Image of the King, which gave them enormous worth and value outside of their individual achievements.

What would your life look like if you treated every person you encountered as the Image bearer that they are? What would look different? List one practical way you could do this just as CS Lewis did.

Finally, rest. Show God that you trust Him. Show God that you understand how magnificent His majesty is and that you truly believe that your worth comes only through *Him* and *His* sacrifice... Simply. By. Resting.

"So then, there remains a Sabbath rest for the people of God, for whoever has entered God's rest has also rested from his works as God did from his. Let us therefore strive to enter that rest, so that no one may fall by the same sort of disobedience."

- Hebrews 4:9-11

Did you see that? *Strive to enter rest.* Usually, rest is something we think of as effortless. You either lay down your head for a few minutes or put up your feet. Not this type of rest. The rest I refer to here is a holy one. A rest that is "set apart" for the glory of God, and to put all your faith and trust in Him, it requires effort.

Name one thing you can strive for that will help you enter a holy rest. It could be a clean room, a restful activity, a person you feel calm around, a way to pray or read the Bible, etc.

The Sabbath is a gift. Reach out your arms and accept it.

. . . .

"The Sabbath was made for man, not man for the Sabbath."

- Mark 2:27

Is there anything that has been stopping you from accepting the Lord's gift of Sabbath?

What I love about this application is that once we have grasped this belief and strive to push out the lies and accept the truth that our identity as image-bearers of God is what makes us worthy, the results are merely a consequence of our beliefs. Following the quote above from Jordan Peterson, he listed a few consequential results that would be attainable if we begin to act as though we were worthy:

- Our lives will be richer, more meaningful, deeper and worthwhile.
- We will strive to educate ourselves and become wiser.
- We will respect ourselves more.
- We will be a better model for others (which is severely underrated nowadays in my opinion).
- We will be a better sister, friend, mother, wife, etc.
- And we will be less ridden with guilt that "we aren't what we could be."
- And we will finally see that we are enough, but only through Him.

Group Questions

1. Everyone shares one thing they often look to for their worth. How has that thing let you down in the past or exposed its inability to ultimately give you satisfaction and value?

2. Is the idea of resting as an act of worship and trust new to you? Discuss some practical steps to start implementing this rest into your life.

3. Why do you think it's so hard for us to fully believe that God gives us value and worth? What is stopping you?

4. Read the list of the results above of acting as though you have worth... does that sound like something you want to have?

5. Are there any other topics or verses that stood out to anyone they would like to further discuss?

Group Blessing

Blessed are you, Lord our God, King of the universe, who has given us worth by calling us by name. Not by our works do we find our value, but through your creation and your sacrifice. Let us glorify you, not only through our work but also through our rest. Bestow upon us the peace that comes with forgiveness. Help us find our value in you alone and let us be lights to those who call themselves "worthless." We praise you for all that you have done and thank you for your gift of rest.

Amen.

Generous

By Addie Parris

Proverbs 31:15,20

She gets up while it is still dark; she provides food for her family and portions her servant girls. She opens her arms to the poor and extends her hands to the needy.

Generous *(adj) 1. (of a person) showing a readiness to give more of something, as money or time, than is strictly necessary or expected. 2. (of a thing) larger or more plentiful than is usual or necessary.*

God Freely Gives

"But go rather to the lost sheep of the house of Israel. And proclaim as you go, saying, The kingdom of heaven is at hand. Heal the sick, raise the dead, cleanse lepers, cast out demons. You received without paying; give without pay."

-Matthew 10:6-8

It's easy to get into the habit of thinking that we are in control of our lives. We think, "it's my life, my room, my car, my clothes." We have the perception that we are in control of our present and our future. However, we aren't as in control as we think we are. In this journey of life, there is a big story at play, and it's not ours.

One of my favorite songs is, *Great are you Lord.* I love the lyrics, "It's your breath in our lungs, so we pour out our praise." It comes from the book of Genesis, where it says God *breathed* His life into us.

"Then the Lord God formed the man of dust from the ground and breathed into his nostrils the breath of life, and the man became a living creature."

– Genesis 2:7

Even our *breath* is not our own. It's God's.

What do you think about this? How does it make you feel to think about our very breath not being our own?

It is He who gives us life. He who made the earth. He who gave intelligence to Marie Curie. He who gave athleticism to Serena Williams, and He who gave creativity to Joanna Gaines. It's all because of Him, and it's all for His glory (Isaiah 43:7). In reality, we are just a small part of this grand story and God graciously lets us be a part of it. We, as followers of Jesus, are called to a greater life and a greater purpose, which is to glorify God and spread the good news of the Gospel (1 Peter 2:9; Matthew 28:19).

List 5 things that you have, either physical or just part of who you are, that you realize are gifts given to you by God:

It is His story at play, not our own. It is His love and abundant grace that has allowed us to live lives of wonder with freedom from our flesh, and thus, we should desire to give what we first received. Out of the overflow of His love for us, we should desire to be like our Creator and become generous with our God-given gifts and time.

We all like the idea of being generous, but in order to do it well, we must realize that nothing in this life belongs to us. It is God's who is in control of all things, who made all things.

If you think about it, it's kind of freeing knowing that nothing in this world belongs to us. I would much rather trust a God who is perfect, sinless, just, and holy to be in charge of all things way before I would trust a sinful, corrupt, impatient, and selfish human like myself to be in control. The Lord provides (Matthew 6:26). Therefore, we don't have to worry about having our needs met or hoarding our resources in case something happens. His supply of our needs is never-ending.

Though the Lord is in control and truly provides for our day to day well-being. He already so generously gave us the most freeing gift there has ever been, which is the gift of Jesus and the cross.

Rewrite that sentence. Contemplate what it means...

We all have fallen short of the glory of God (Romans 3:23) and deserve eternal separation from Him. We had a problem that we could not fix on our own (again, see how we are not in control?). But God, abounding in love for us, sent a way for our redemption. He sent His only Son to save us. Jesus, the man who knew no sin, did what we could never do for ourselves. As said in Hebrews 12:2, "For the joy set before him he (Jesus) endured the cross, scorning its shame." Jesus went to the cross willingly for our sake. Despite being betrayed by His closest friends, mocked, spat on, beaten, and having to go through separation from God... He still did it.

Jesus took away our sins and washed us white as snow. He so generously gave us grace and poured His love out to us on the cross.

In Matthew 10:8, it says, "Freely you have received, freely give." What Jesus did was a free gift and all we have to do is say yes to it. Because of that, we are able to freely give our own gifts to others.

Recap this section in your own words. How can the truth "God Freely Gives" help us be generous?

Personal Story

When I think of the people whose generosity has impacted me the most, I don't think of anything monetary.

Instead, I think of the people in my life who let me cry on them when I went through a breakup or didn't get the college acceptance letter I was hoping for. They didn't say anything. They simply gave me their presence and time.

I think of how an older and wiser friend literally took me everywhere with her. She brought me to the grocery store, family parties, and dates with her boyfriend. Sometimes, I would even sit on the lid of the toilet and talk to her while she was in the shower.

What was most profound about those times is that they weren't profound at all. It was nothing fancy. There were no big events or outings. Yet, that time showed me so much of what it looked like to follow Christ. She did this by generously allowing me into mundane parts of her life and giving me so much of her time.

There is a married couple in my life that allowed me into their home and pretty much adopted me into their family. Getting to watch them love each other, fight, offer grace, and start a family was where my desire to be a wife and a mom started to grow, a desire that God had planted in my heart since I was a little girl. Only a few couples let others into the messy parts of relationships. However, after generously allowing me to have an inside look at what marriage and having a family is like, my life changed forever.

I also think of the people who came alongside me as I went through a season of crippling anxiety. They generously gave up their time to pray with me and for me. They were always there to hug me and let me cry as I woke up anxious almost every morning. They listened as I shared all the thoughts consuming my head when they had plenty of other things to do or problems of their own. They helped carry my burdens without complaint.

. . . .

"Carry each other's burdens, and in this way you will fulfill the law of Christ."

– Galatians 6:2

The opposite of being generous is being selfish, and as followers of Jesus, there's no room for that. Paul wrote to his friend, Timothy, about this subject saying:

"People will be lovers of themselves, lovers of money, boastful, proud, abusive, disobedient to their parents, ungrateful, unholy, without love, unforgiving, slanderous, without self-control, brutal, not lovers of the good, treacherous, rash, conceited, lovers of pleasure rather than lovers of God."

- 2 Timothy 3:2-4

The world tells us it is okay to be selfish. We're told to only look after ourselves and our own interests. However, as Christians, we are told not to conform to the patterns of this world (Romans 12:2). We are supposed to look different!

Application

So, what does it mean to be generous? What if being generous didn't just have financial implications? What if it meant giving your time? Your presence? A listening ear? A shoulder to cry on? A bed to sleep in?

What areas of your life are you currently generous?

Society's definition of being generous usually centers around money. We're told to tithe to our church, give to mission trips, or donate to foundations, which are all great things! But in this season of life, when we're still young, perhaps still dependent on our parents, and trying to figure out God's plan and calling on our lives, maybe we should think outside of the box for possible ways to be generous.

So, what are some practical ways to live out being generous?

In my own life, it means the world to me when people take the time to ask about how my day was and don't accept "good" as an answer. I love it when people really take the time to listen to the deeper parts of my heart; my hopes, my dreams, my fears, and my wounds. Having others listen to me has blessed me tremendously, and it has made me want to bless others in the same way.

There is a deep longing inside each of us to be heard and known. So, if you want to love others, generously offer a listening ear to whatever it is they have to say. Ask someone how their day was and actually engage in the conversation. Be that person. Step in.

"Opening your arms to the poor and giving to the needy" (vs. 20) doesn't always mean handing out money to the homeless man on the street corner, which by no means is a bad thing to do. But what if the "needy" are the people who desperately long for someone to genuinely care about what they're going through? What if the "poor" is your friend who just needs a warm bed to sleep in for a night because their home life isn't the best, even if it means sleeping on the floor?

Have you ever been presented with this type of situation where someone was poor or needy either physically, emotionally or spiritually? What was your response?

Maybe in our case, as single girls, providing food for your family as it talks about in verse 15 could mean making dinner for your parents, or making a home-cooked meal for your roommates who have a long night of studying ahead of them.

There are so many simple ways to be generous. Be creative! It could be something as little as letting your roommate borrow a dryer sheet for her laundry, or letting your little sister use your nail polish.

. . . .

"Dear children, let us not love with words or speech but with actions and in truth."

- 1 John 3:18

Let us rejoice in the fact that Jesus has given you and I the best gift we could ever receive in the Cross. It is because of His sacrifice that grace is freely poured out on us over and over again.

In the definition of generous, it says, "showing a readiness to give more of something." Jesus is always ready to show you more of how much He loves you, how He fights for you and pursues you. His love for you will never run dry and His grace will never run out. Praise the Lord!

What if we took all the qualities in the passage of 2nd Timothy and did the opposite? What if instead of...

Loving ourselves...we loved others.

Loving money...we loved to give it away.

Boasting... we were humble.

Proud...we were meek.

Abusive...we were gentle.

Unforgiving...we were gracious.

*Circle the above words on the left that you struggle with,
and write down a few practical ways to look more like the right side of the list!*

If we want to be true lovers of God, the scriptures say we must be the latter.

Not only this, but the scriptures also say that we *ourselves* will be blessed by being generous to others!

" A generous person will prosper;
whoever refreshes others will be refreshed. "

– Proverbs 11:25

Rewrite this verse.

Group Questions

1. Do you truly believe that you have received the greatest gift of all time?

2. What are some things that hold you back from being generous?

3. List 5-10 ways to be generous that does not involve money.

Group Blessing

God, we thank you for all you have given us. From the breath in our lungs to the possessions we own, to the important people in our lives. We ask that you give us the desire to give to others as freely as you have given us. Help us not be stingy with our time, possessions and resources. Change our mindsets to desire to give no matter the cost and give me the energy and strength to do so.

Amen.

Fearless

By Anastasia Jones

Proverbs 31:21, 25

When it snows, she has no fear for her household; for all of them are clothed in scarlet. She can laugh at the days to come.

Fearless *(a) 1. Being FREE from fear.*

God is faithful

"The Lord himself goes before you and will be with you; he will never leave you nor forsake you. Do not be afraid; do not be discouraged."

–Deuteronomy 31:8

Who goes ahead of you?

365. Not only does this number represent the number of days it takes for the earth to revolve around the sun, it also represents the number of times "do not fear" phrases are written in the Bible. That's right! There are 365 "do not fear" phrases in the Word of God, one for every day of the calendar year!

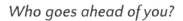

"Say to those who have an anxious heart, 'Be strong; fear not! Behold, your God will come with vengeance, with the recompense of God. He will come and save you.'"

–Isaiah 35:4

"Even though I walk through the valley of the shadow of death, I will fear no evil, for you are with me; your rod and your staff, they comfort me."

–Psalm 23:4

"The LORD is my light and my salvation; whom shall I fear?
The LORD is the stronghold of my life;
of whom shall I be afraid?"

-Psalm 27:1

Now I know how easy it can be to read facts like this and think, "hmm, that's interesting," and then write it off as some sort of cosmic coincidence or fun fact you found beneath the cap of a Snapple iced-tea bottle. However, if I know one thing to be true about our God, it's that there is always a divine power, purpose, and plan within every word He speaks. Could it be that this specific repetition was for a reason?

How would you define "fearless"?

The Miriam Webster Dictionary defines being fearless as being "free from fear: Brave." Other synonyms for fearless include: bold, courageous, gutsy and my personal favorite - lionhearted. I find it interesting that fearless is not defined as "being without fear" but being "free" from it. We may still feel the emotional and physiological effects of fear, but when we are fearless, we become free from them. When we are fearless, we no longer allow fear to hold us back from taking the right action. Regardless of the challenges our circumstances present, we refuse to be left behind, thereby resolving to move forward into the unknown. We take a leap of faith because *God is faithful.*

"Know therefore that the LORD your God is God, the faithful God
who keeps covenant and steadfast love with those who love him and
keep his commandments, to a thousand generations,"

-Deuteronomy 7:9

"If we are faithless, he remains faithful,
for he cannot deny Himself."

-2 Timothy 2:13

One of the greatest leaps of faith in the Old Testament was made by Queen Esther. Soon after her rise to royalty, the entire existence of her people was threatened by a man with a sinister plot to eradicate the Jews from existence. Although Mordecai, her cousin, discovered the cruel plan of Haman, he did not have the power to interrupt the course of events that would eventually lead to the mass genocide of his people. However, he knew that his cousin, Esther, did.

"Then Mordecai told them to reply to Esther, "Do not think to yourself that in the king's palace you will escape any more than all the other Jews. For if you keep silent at this time, relief and deliverance will rise for the Jews from another place, but you and your father's house will perish. And who knows whether you have not come to the kingdom for such a time as this?" Then Esther told them to reply to Mordecai, "Go, gather all the Jews to be found in Susa, and hold a fast on my behalf, and do not eat or drink for three days, night or day. I and my young women will also fast as you do. Then I will go to the king, though it is against the law, and if I perish, I perish." Mordecai then went away and did everything as Esther had ordered him."

-Esther 4:13-17

Through a series of secret messages exchanged back and forth between Esther and her cousin, there was a pivotal moment that took place in Chapter 4, somewhere between verses 14 and 15 that changed the course of history forever.

Retell this story of Esther in your own words.

Oftentimes, our greatest acts of fearlessness begin in the quiet moments. Like a single spark that fans into a brilliant flame, it was in this moment of fearless clarity that Esther resolved to go before the king (a bold decision that she knew could result in her immediate death, and consequently, the death of her people).

What I appreciate most about Esther is her God-fearing strategy for the future. She didn't just take a blind leap of faith. Instead, she followed her fearless decision with a series of divine directives for herself and her people. She understood the magnitude of what was at stake and she knew she needed to consecrate herself for this mighty task. God was faithful to her all the days of her life, and she relied on His faithfulness as she carried out her calling. After assembling all the Jews in Susa for three days of intense prayer and fasting, Esther boldly stood before the king with a God-given boldness that led to the salvation of her tribe.

Write: "I can be fearless because God is faithful."

Esther did not allow the fear of the future to frighten her from being fearless in the present. She knew that God's people were too precious for Him to allow this to happen, and her recently attained status was indeed for a divine purpose. In 4:15, Esther confidently took her leap of faith with the fearless belief that God would be faithful to her, and she laughed at the days to come!

We become fearless because we have the belief that God is faithful. It's hard to make that leap when you don't know if you will be caught. Be assured *you will be.*

Do you believe God is faithful?

"God is faithful, by whom you were called into the fellowship of his Son, Jesus Christ our Lord."

-1 Corinthians 1:9

Recap this section in your own words. How can the truth, "God is Faithful" help us be fearless?

Personal Story

Full disclosure – I have a thing with heights. We don't really get along.

We've been trying to work it out over the past few years, but things aren't really progressing as quickly as I'd like. My friends are aware of this, which is why my adventure buddy, Noah, peer pressured me to go skydiving with him a few years back. Now, I can't quite recall specifically, but I'm sure my gut reaction to his outlandish request was a very decisive and quick-witted "no." But Noah has always been persistent and was not about to take no for an answer. He not only encouraged me to face my fear but also encouraged me to catch it on camera. A true friend.

Now, I know you aren't able to watch the said video as you're reading this chapter, so I'll do my best to describe to you the most emotionally exhausting 20 minutes of my life thus far.

I went into the experience with an inordinate amount of energy. I really didn't need a hype man because I was my own hype man. It was happening, and I was here for it. Everything turned when that hollow metal airplane rolled up on the tarmac. I stepped into that plane with about 50% confidence in the plan, and each second that passed wasn't helping my numbers. As we ascended to the tune of 10,000 feet, all I could think about was the fact that even if I could scream, no one would hear me. And even if they did hear me, they surely wouldn't give me a refund...or would they? Don't worry. I didn't test my theory. Instead, I sat uncommonly frozen and let the seconds pass like hours as I and waited for my confrontation with heights to commence.

When we reached altitude, they swung the door open and beckoned me and my tandem jumper toward it. I went forward a bit reluctantly since I was absolutely terrified. As I swung my legs over the edge, at the perfectly symmetrical view below, I quite literally thought my entire life would be over as soon as I jumped. I'd like to say I knew it would be a long way down, but I actually didn't. I thought that the moment I jumped, I would immediately hit the ground.

So, I jumped. I jumped before I could start running through what the headlines in the newspapers would say about my tragic death. "A tragic case of a Groupon gone terribly wrong." I jumped before I contemplated fighting for a refund. If I'm honest, I jumped because deep down, I wanted the adventure. I craved it. I desperately wanted to have a story to tell. I wanted to push the limits of what I thought I could do. I jumped because I was curious to see what would happen if I did.

In our society, fearlessness is made to seem loud, strong, bold; but in many ways, fearlessness may actually feel more like a quiet curiosity that creeps its way into the back of your mind as you wonder what the future would be like if you did take a step. Then with a little courage, that quiet curiosity gives way to action without an expectation of the end result, and that action may even turn into wonder as your faith in God's hand on your future unfolds in a way that becomes better than you could ever have imagined.

When we are free from fear, we are full of faith! We declare that we are safe in His wings. Seen in His eyes. Wrapped in His love. This is what gives us the confidence to step into the unknown with courage. This is the beginning of a never-ending adventure! This is what grounds us in the midst of the ambiguity.

Application

When we allow our actions to be dictated by fear, it keeps us from experiencing all the good and perfect things that God wants to do in and through us. When we operate out of a place of fear, we choose to keep ourselves from the calling that God has for us. Fear keeps us stuck in the past, and from our calling.

Write about a time that fear held you back from what you felt you were supposed to do.

Many of the fearless decisions we make in our life will be made without an audience. They will be decided in ordinary places, whether within the comfort of your own home, sitting alone at a coffee shop, walking down the street to the corner store, or sitting at a bench in the park on your lunch break.

Acts of fearlessness aren't always preceded by a loud battle cry but in the small moments. Often, fearless decisions are made when no one is looking. Applying for the job, quitting the job, launching the business, writing a book, becoming your own boss, moving half-way across the world, making new friends, forgiving old ones. This is one of the reasons I love the story of Esther. Here, Esther is faced with the tragic news of the eminent mass genocide of her people. Her decision to enter the presence of the king and save her people was not made with a grand audience.

Now that we've spent some time talking about what fearlessness IS, let's take a minute to talk about what it is NOT. *Fearlessness is NOT recklessness.*

Write: "fearlessness is not recklessness."

Now, I know some would say that the act of jumping out of a perfectly good airplane is reckless behavior but hear me out:

Recklessness is defined in the Merriam-Webster dictionary as "marked by lack of proper caution: careless of consequences. Irresponsible."

Fearlessness is defined as "free from fear. Brave."

Now, let me tell you something about skydiving...there is absolutely nothing reckless about it. I say this because, in order to become a certified skydiver, it requires a crazy amount of hands-on training. I mean the amount of skill, time and expertise that goes into skydiving is utterly insane. Someone can't simply jump out of a plane a couple of times and call themselves a skydiver. It takes skill and a lot of tandem/guided jumps to be qualified for the lowest possible level of skydiving. There is nothing "irresponsible" or "careless" about it.

Every moment spent being briefed by the team and running through skydiving protocol gave me the reassurance I needed when it was my turn to jump, even though I was afraid…terrified, even. Sure, in the moments before I jumped, I said a few prayers, "just in case." But truthfully, I jumped because I believed that the person in tandem with me knew what they were doing and that he had everything under control. I believed that the skilled skydiver with me had contingency plans where I had confusion. I believed that he knew what he was doing, so no matter what, I would be safe.

What if being fearless doesn't mean being entirely without fear? What if being fearless means having enough faith to simply being FREE from fear and no longer being bound by its paralyzing chains? Take your leap of faith out of the plane with the fearless belief that God will be faithful to catch you.

I love this letter that author Elizabeth Gilbert wrote in her book, Big Magic

"Dearest Fear: Creativity and I are about to go on a road trip together. I understand you'll be joining us because you always do. I acknowledge that you believe you have an important job to do in my life and that you take your job seriously. Apparently, your job is to induce complete panic whenever I'm about to do anything interesting—and, may I say, you are superb at your job. So, by all means, keep doing your job, if you feel you must. But I will also be doing my job on this road trip, which is to work hard and stay focused. And Creativity will be doing its job, which is to remain stimulating and inspiring. There's plenty of room in this vehicle for all of us, so make yourself at home, but understand this: Creativity and I are the only ones who will be making any decisions along the way. I recognize and respect that you are part of this family, and so I will never exclude you from our activities, but still—your suggestions will never be followed. You're allowed to have a seat, and you're allowed to have a voice, but you are not allowed to have a vote. You're not allowed to touch the road maps; you're not allowed to suggest detours; you're not allowed to fiddle with the temperature. Dude, you're not even allowed to touch the radio. But above all else, my dear old familiar friend, you are absolutely forbidden to drive."

– Elizabeth Gilbert, Big Magic: Creative Living Beyond Fear [c]

Elizabeth Gilbert did not write this from a Christian perspective, so let's substitute "Creativity" with "The Holy Spirit." What if we give fearless permission to the Holy Spirit to drive on this journey through life? Let fear take a back seat, maybe offer the occasional cautious word, but never let it hijack the wheel from the one who really should be in control.

Are you ready to be free from your fear? First, you must start by giving the wheel to the Holy Spirit.

Naming your fear can help you overcome it. What is something you are constantly afraid of? Find a pattern, and call it out.

Now, as you continue your fearless journey, I want to encourage you! The number of fearless decisions you make can have a direct correlation to the calling God has for you. Think about David facing Goliath, or Esther facing the King, or Ruth leaving her homeland to honor her Mother-in-Law. These are all massive steps these people made towards God's calling for their lives and they all started with one fearless step. His plans for us hardly involve being comfortable, secure, and at peace with the things of this earth. While fear can keep us out of some terrible situations, it can also keep us from embracing wonderful opportunities that have been placed before us. Don't let fear keep you from your best future. Here are some of my favorite mantras to encourage fearlessness.

"God's plan is greater than mine."

"The fun is in the mystery."

"Worst case scenario, it's ALL in His hands, and this is going to be an epic story to tell one day."

Group Questions

1. What things have you been putting off "until tomorrow" because of fear?

2. How can we take on the belief that God is faithful to help free us from our fears?

3. Name one practical step you will take this week towards fearlessness.

Group Blessing

God, we acknowledge your faithfulness throughout all generations. We thank you for your consistency and your everlasting love. You are steadfast, unending, and unfailing. We ask that you instill the peace that comes from your faithful love and allow us to do fearless acts in your name. Call us into something beyond ourselves and challenge us to be fearless. Give us your strength to do so.

Amen.

Diligent & Enterprising

By April Pryor

Proverbs 31:14-16, 18, 24

She is like the merchant ships, bringing her food from afar. She gets up while it is still night; she provides food for her family and portions for her female servants. She considers a field and buys it; out of her earnings she plants a vineyard. She sees that her trading is profitable, and her lamp does not go out at night. She makes linen garments and sells them, and supplies the merchants with sashes.

Diligent *(a) 1. Having or showing care and taking painstaking or particular care in one's work or duties.*

Enterprising *(a) 1. Having or showing initiative; able to deal skillfully and promptly with new situations or difficulties.*

God is our source

Do you find it hard to care about your work sometimes? Whether it's chores around the house, schoolwork, that phone call you've been putting off or just plain keeping your room or car clean, sometimes it's hard to find the desire or energy to do it well. If someone isn't looking over our shoulders telling us how to do it better, we might just do it half-way to get on with whatever it is that we deem more important at the moment. I mean, Netflix isn't going to watch itself! We might struggle with taking on responsibility, but it is a lot easier to let *other* people take on roles that give them the accountability that is often associated with responsibility.

Talk about a situation where this is a consistent struggle for you.

In these verses of Proverbs 31, we see a woman taking the initiative of her responsibilities. People depend on her to do her work. It takes forethought and intentionality to be prepared for the day that awaits her. She is considerate, which shows us that she takes time to think things through before she makes a decision. When she earns money, she spends it on things that have a lasting effect. She makes sure that what she is spending her money on is worth it! We also see her working with her hands to earn money. And how about those sashes?!

How did she get there? How did she mature into the ability to take all this on? Why does she care so deeply about making long-term investments? How does she know what to do next? In order for us to move forward with God's design, we need His strength because HE IS OUR SOURCE! He will strengthen us and show us the right way!

Rewrite that last sentence.

*"On the day I called, you answered me;
my strength of soul you increased."*

-Psalm 138:3

*"If the Spirit of him who raised Jesus from the dead dwells in you,
he who raised Christ Jesus from the dead will also give life to your
mortal bodies through his Spirit who dwells in you."*

-Romans 8:11

*"I am the vine; you are the branches. Whoever abides in me and
I in him, he it is that bears much fruit, for apart from me you
can do nothing."*

-John 15:5

(This entire chapter of John is a great picture of living in Him as our source).

Pick one of the above verses to rewrite in your own words.

First, we must admit that we can't do it all and that we do need to get ideas or energy from elsewhere sometimes. There are a lot of places we can go to learn or get more information. We might go to a book or the internet to get such information. Pinterest has some nice ideas, and YouTube has great how-to videos. In an age where we have so much information at our fingertips, it is very important as Christians to remember that God is our number one source and that He wrote us a letter! He has taught us how to live, ways to treat people and He revealed His plans through the Bible. Dive into the Word. Get to know the Lord through how He describes Himself and the ways He views you.

What do you think it means for the Lord to be your source?

Then, we need to be willing to put ourselves in a situation that would challenge us to face something unknown. That might feel scary or unpredictable. But it's in these moments that we can mature and grow. We can face a challenge and rise to the occasion; It might be facing a task that is not necessarily new to you, such as chores, dealing with a difficult friendship or relationship, etc., but what might become different this time would probably be your attitude towards the task. You could decide to face the same task without complaining and doing it with pristine excellence.

God will meet you where you are! He sees you and knows you! He is *not surprised* by your circumstances, your personality, your family situation or your limitations. He is always ready to take a willing heart who has claimed Him as Lord and work with it.

Write: "God is not surprised by my circumstances. He created my personality and he knows about my situation. My limitations are so I can rely on Him."

Maybe you've heard the phrase, "God doesn't give you more than you can handle." It actually doesn't say that anywhere in the Bible. What it does say is that when you are given more than you can handle, God is right there to give you the strength to continue! (2 Corinthians 1:8-9) In fact, we should count it as a blessing to encounter a problem too big for us to solve because then we are forced to rely on Him! (Matthew 5:3, MSG)

. . . .

"Trust in the Lord with all your heart, and do not lean on your own understanding. In all your ways acknowledge him, and he will make straight your paths."

- Proverbs 3:5-6

"I will say to the Lord, "My refuge and my fortress, my God, in whom I trust."

-Psalm 91:2

"For as the heavens are higher than the earth, so are my ways higher than your ways and my thoughts than your thoughts."

-Isaiah 55:9d

"The Lord is righteous in all his ways and kind in all his works."

-Psalm 145:17

Recap this section in your own words. How can the truth "God is my Source" help us be Diligent and Enterprising?

Personal Story

When I was in college, I went on a mission trip to Jamaica to work at a summer camp for the deaf. My experience there awoke something in me that I didn't know was there; a LOVE to communicate with my hands and to work with deaf people. I came home after a month of serving and couldn't wait to go back the next year! I knew I needed to take more sign language classes in order to be able to communicate better the next year. So, I took the initiative and started looking around the area where I was in college and found a community college that offered classes. While I was there and taking my class, I found out that people were there to become trained as sign language interpreters!! I was so excited, and after some prayer and seeking wisdom from my parents, I decided to enroll for a degree! I took action, and I found out which of my classes I had already taken for my Business undergraduate degree would transfer to the new school. I picked up extra hours at my job to pay for the new expenses of the new degree I was taking on. I found a church for the deaf in my area and started attending their services so I could learn more about deaf culture. I ended up graduating 2 years in a row, one with my business degree and the next with my 2-year degree in Manual Communications.

Through this whole process, I was faced with lots of new situations and decisions I needed to make or figure out. I would consult my parents on the decision-making pieces, and they helped guide me through those times. On the practical side, I had to figure out how to get to my new school (remember, this is before the days of cell phones and google maps!) and find out where to park in a downtown, inner-city setting. I had to think ahead and plan what to pack to eat since I was gone from home for lunch and dinner most days and was super poor, so eating out wasn't an option. I had to budget my income carefully so that I could pay my school bills on time as I was determined not to go into debt for this second degree. My skill in *enterprising* grew greatly in those years. I discovered something I LOVED, something God had put inside me that was waking up. I had the energy and motivation to figure out what it was that needed to be done.

At the moment, I was just moving forward with what I felt was before me. Now, I see that the things I learned about being enterprising and diligent in my single years prepared me greatly for my married life and mothering my 5 kids. Sometimes it's hard to see at the moment how what we are learning or the ways the Lord is challenging us might help us in the years to come, but I can tell you from experience: He is constantly challenging us for our growth that we might not even see for 5+ years! Persevere and continue to draw from Him as your source and you'll reap the sweet fruit in the years to come.

Have you been in a situation like this or considered an opportunity similar to April, but not gone through with it? If so, why do you think that was? If, for any reason, it was a lack in your diligence, pray about it right now. Give it to the Lord. Call on Him to give you the strength and endurance for what He's calling you to.

Application

In these verses, we see our Proverbs 31 lady doing some grown-up things that make it hard to understand her or relate to her. But if you break it down into **diligence** and **enterprising**, it helps us see some pretty cool things that could help us become more godly ladies. And after all, that's what it's all about, right?

Take **Enterprising,** for example. The dictionary defines it as *"Having or showing initiative; able to deal skillfully and promptly with new situations or difficulties."*

Think about a task or responsibility in your life that someone has to nag you to do.

This could be a practical task, like getting your oil changed, or an emotional or relational task like praying more intentionally or investing in a relationship. Name whatever it is here.

It's funny how those things don't take care of themselves! I challenge you to make a decision to show initiative about that situation. Take action on it before you get reminded about it. Once you've sufficiently dealt with it, think of one or two other things you usually neglect until prodded. When you struggle or grumble, ask our Source, The Lord Jesus, for help. What this looks like for me is when I start to feel overwhelmed, bored, anxious or frustrated, I've trained myself to say, "Jesus! Help me, please." By saying that phrase, it reminds my brain and turns my heart towards Him. I may not really mean it quite yet or know exactly how He's going to help me, but my heart has to be reminded that there is a source outside of myself that I can call upon. It starts a conversation with Him. Jesus' name is the name above every other name! (Phil. 2:9)

Do you believe that?

His name is powerful. Uttering it in a moment of desperation or pain or lack of motivation can shift our focus off ourselves and onto Him. Then, the next thing I usually say is something like, "What is it that you have for me? I want what you want." It's an act of surrender. It helps me lay down whatever I was struggling with and allow Him to work in and through my heart. Now, this doesn't mean you'll hear a voice or something. Instead it might just be something like an idea popping into your head of how to tackle the task before you or being filled with a peace that will un-paralyze you and allow you to move forward. It can also be a renewed sense of purpose coming over you that will help you understand the "why" behind what you need to do. Before you know it, you will be able to take on new things with skill and promptness. You will take ownership of your days and time.

Does this sound like something you can do? If not, how come? What's holding you back?

A nice pairing with enterprising is **Diligence**. The definition is *"Having or showing care and taking painstaking or particular care in one's work or duties."* Did you notice how our Proverbs 31 friend cares about what she does? She seems to have ideas about what it's going to take for her to accomplish the responsibilities and tasks placed before her. Now, let's think about that responsibility that we mentioned earlier that you have to be prodded to do. How could you take particular care in your work or duty related to it? I challenge you to *own* it!

Embracing these kinds of ideas, like noticing things that need to be done and taking it upon yourself to do them when no one is watching, might require us to do a little bit of dying to ourselves.

"And he said to all, "If anyone would come after me, let him deny himself and take up his cross daily and follow me."

-Luke 9:23

"And those who belong to Christ Jesus have crucified the flesh with its passions and desires."

-Galatians 5:24

Is the phrase "die to yourself" new to you? If so, read the verses above a few times and maybe even read them in their full context to see what the writers were talking about. This is something frequently asked of Christians, to put others and God's will first before ourselves. This is often called "dying to ourselves" or putting our selfish desires to death so that God's righteous will might be put in priority.

Dying to ourselves or denying ourselves might not naturally occur to us. We will have to sacrifice something in order to do that; like our time and energy and mind space. Not only does this prepare you for your potential future as a hard worker, employee, wife, mother and household manager, and all that will require of you, it will also draw you closer to the SOURCE. When we can't do it on our own, that's GOOD! It means we need the Lord to help us make it through. When we have to say no to our selfish ideas, or the things we'd rather be doing, it is great preparation and practice for loving the body of Christ well.

"I have been crucified with Christ. It is no longer I who live, but Christ who lives in me. And the life I now live in the flesh I live by faith in the Son of God, who loved me and gave himself for me."

–Galatians 2:20

Group Questions

1. What type of task or responsibility do you frequently flake off on? (Don't be embarrassed, everyone has something!) Do you want to improve in that area?

2. How do you think you might go about relying on and calling upon the Lord to be your source in all things?

3. Do you believe that the hard times are actually a blessing since we get to rely on God and draw closer to Him? If not, discuss what holds you back.

4. Do you agree that it's important to surrender your will to the Lord's will? This might include not giving in to a prideful or lazy nature. If you truly believe it's important, then discuss the implications of that belief in your everyday life.

Group Blessing

Lord, we thank you for being everything we cannot be. Your will is higher than our will, and your ways are higher than our ways. We repent from the pride of resisting your strength. We cannot do it on our own and we surrender to your loving arms as we draw from you as our source. We thank you for helping and strengthening us in all things and we ask you to direct our steps toward the tasks you have in mind for us. We want to do those tasks with a willing and diligent spirit.

Amen.

Driven

By Naomi Fierro

Proverbs 31:17,19

She sets about her work vigorously; her arms are strong for her tasks. In her hand she holds the distaff and grasps the spindle with her fingers.

Driven (a) 1. (of a person) relentlessly compelled by the need to accomplish a goal; very hard-working and ambitious. 2. Motivated or determined by a specified factor or feeling. 3. operated, moved, or controlled by a specified person or source of power

God is trustworthy

I want you to think about the last time you were really driven to do something. *What propelled you to take action?* It's because you either convinced yourself, or someone else convinced you to do it for whatever reason, right? There was an active force of reason that was rooted in a strong belief that pushed you into a drive. There was a purpose, a goal and maybe even a person behind that.

When was the last time you were driven to take action on something? What caused you to do so?

When we look at the word *driven*, we see in the definition above that it means to be moved by something or motivated by something. In order to move you, you must be fully convinced of its worthwhileness, right? So, we could say that being driven by something at its root is simply how deeply you believe in it.

I want to pitch the idea that at the root of being *driven* by God and being *driven* in life, we have to completely surrender in wholehearted faith to God and faith in the plans He has for our lives. We must believe that He is trustworthy. Without that faith, we will become a passive, unmotivated generation with zero *drive* for life. Or even worse, we will be driven by the wrong things.

So, what does faith or trust have to do with being driven?

If we look into the Old Testament, we see that when certain characters of faith decide to take action, it is because they knew what story they were a part of, and it wasn't their own. We live in a culture where people desperately want to believe they are the author and main character of their own story. We think that if we are the author of our lives, then we can "take control of our destiny" and make everything happen the way we want it to be, or that we can propel ourselves into the future we want to be in. It's a very self-centered way to live. But that isn't the story the Bible is telling us. From the very start, the first book, the first verse... "In the beginning, God created the heavens and the earth." Who do we see pop up at the beginning of the story? It doesn't say, "So, this is how humans were made." The Bible is very clear that we are living in a *God-centered story.*

Characters like Abel, Noah, Abraham, Rahab & Anna all knew that they were living in God's story. For me, this bit of the story of Rahab, in particular, stands out the most. If you are unfamiliar with the story, the Israelites were being sent into the Promised Land by the Lord to defeat a city named Jericho. It was an evil city and the Israelites sent spies ahead. While they were there, they almost got caught but a prostitute named Rahab hid them from the guards. She explains why she did so, saying:

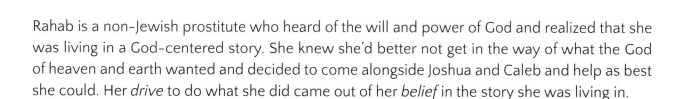

"*I know that the Lord has given you this land and that a great fear of you has fallen on us, so that all who live in this country are melting in fear because of you. We have heard how the Lord dried up the water of the Red Sea for you when you came out of Egypt, and what you did to Sihon and Og, the two kings of the Amorites east of the Jordan, whom you completely destroyed. When we heard of it, our hearts melted in fear and everyone's courage failed because of you, for the Lord your God is God in heaven above and on the earth below.*"

- Joshua 2:9-11

Rahab is a non-Jewish prostitute who heard of the will and power of God and realized that she was living in a God-centered story. She knew she'd better not get in the way of what the God of heaven and earth wanted and decided to come alongside Joshua and Caleb and help as best she could. Her *drive* to do what she did came out of her *belief* in the story she was living in.

Guess who Rahab's great-great-something-grandson was? It was Jesus. This Gentile prostitute was rewarded for her faith and her deep belief in the story in which she lived by getting to be an ancestor to the Messiah. WOW! I mean, that's pretty crazy.

Nearly every time the word *faith* is used in scripture, we can take that word and look at how the Greek translates it in context. That translation comes out to be the word *Pistis*, which means "firm persuasion." "Firm persuasion in what?" you might ask. Firm persuasion by the story God is telling, by the fact that you are not the main character, and that His will and heart are trustworthy. He is worthy of your faith and so is the story He is writing.

Read these verses in Hebrews, Chapter 11. This is a chapter all about believers who went before us with faith to do crazy things for God:

*"By faith, we understand that
the universe was formed at God's command*

By faith, Abel brought God a better offering than Cain did.

By faith Noah, when warned about things not yet seen,

*By faith Abraham, when called to go to a place he would later
receive as his inheritance, obeyed and went."*

Now replace it with the Greek translation and read it like this:

*"By persuasion, we understand that
the universe was formed at God's command*

By persuasion, Abel brought God a better offering than Cain did.

By persuasion Noah, when warned about things not yet seen,

*By persuasion Abraham, when called to go to a place he would
later receive as his inheritance, obeyed and went."*

Woah, this is mind-blowing, right? Noah, Abel and Abraham were persuaded by the story God was telling. God invited them into a story bigger than themselves; one that demonstrated His unfailing love and glorified Him above all else. Through persuasion by the trustworthy heart of God, Abel offered a sacrifice that cost him the firstborn lamb in order to bring Him glory. In faith, Noah built the ark, despite the ridicule of the entire population of earth. Abraham, through persuasion in The Story God was telling, left his homeland for an unfamiliar and far off land in pursuit of God's promises. Faith has to come from somewhere and a belief has to come from something. It comes from persuasion by the heart of God in His Story.

By "Heart of God," I mean God's will and desires. When people say, "follow your heart," they mean "follow what you want to do deep down." Same thing for God, except His heart is perfect. Our hearts can't always be trusted! But his can. His will is sovereign, and His desires are pure. You can trust Him.

Name a few things you have faith or "full persuasion" in.

Do you believe God is trustworthy? Why or why not?

C.S. Lewis has this great quote: "Faith is the art of holding onto things your reason has accepted, in spite of your changing moods." This means that no matter how you feel at the moment, your faith is holding true. This is essential when it comes to being driven because the word "Driven" itself implies that something is driving you. If that thing driving you is your faith in God's story, then it has no need to falter. Faith holds on despite the seasons and the moods. So, the real question is, how deeply do you believe that you live in a God-centered story?

Recap this section in your own words. How can the truth "God is trustworthy" help us be driven?

Personal Story

I remember going on a mission trip some years ago, and it was an incredible time. Everyone on my team had so much *drive* and we all seemed to share a vision and were working towards the same goal; to help the orphans and love the broken with our whole heart. You could say that my team was ON FIRE for God. However, when we got back, some of those people completely lost their *drive*. Not only did they lose their drive for missions and ministry, but they also lost their drive to live a life for God. *So, what happened?*

They were no longer actively being persuaded by the heart of God. They forgot they were living in a God-centered story, or maybe they didn't believe it deeply enough. And because of that, they lost sight of God's visions and promises for their life. They lost faith and stopped establishing, stopped building the ark, stopped bringing the sacrifices, and they stopped believing.

God had a vision for my friends to go into a third-world-nation to fill their hearts with compassion, so they can bring it back to their home and learn how to radically love and serve the community around them. Instead, they stopped connecting to that vision.

The truth is simple. If you don't believe that God has a plan and vision for your life, you will not be persuaded, and you will have no purpose to be driven.

Have you ever felt super "on fire" for Jesus? Like after church camp or when you first encountered Jesus, and you with all your friends decide you want to change the world and preach the gospel to everyone? Or you've been living a double-life, and you decide that you are finally "all in for Jesus" and that the party days are over? But then life happens, and you get back into the groove of life. However, it's easy, far too easy to go back to the life you lived before Jesus. Then, you suddenly have zero drive to run after God.

That's because you quit believing that you're a part of God's story.

. . . .

"The Lord is not slow in keeping his promise, as some understand slowness. Instead he is patient with you, not wanting anyone to perish, but everyone to come to repentance."

- 2 Peter 3:9

"You need to persevere so that when you have done the will of God, you will receive what he has promised."

–Hebrews 10:36

What makes me sad about those friends of mine who lost sight of God's vision is that they didn't persevere or believe that God wanted them to be a part of His Story. This 2 Peter verse is so powerful because it tells us his heart; how he *wants* everyone to come to repentance, and so he *will* be patient. We need only to repent and persevere. What does perseverance require? **A drive.**

Do you feel connected to the heart of God? Are you persuaded simply enough by the fact that our God is trustworthy that you can be driven, or do you easily lose sight of that? How did that come to be?

Application

The sad truth is that we live in a culture where, on one hand, complacency is REAL. But on the other hand, false stories are constantly driving people right off the edge of a cliff.

Which one do you resonate with more? Are you quick to settle for average and comfort? Or are you being driven by a story other than the one God is writing? Both paths are very normal, just so you know. I guarantee you that everyone you know is either one or the other, so don't feel crazy. BUT that doesn't mean it's God's will. So, let's work on setting our eyes on the Lord, aligning our hearts with His will, and believing we are living in a God-centered story.

So, no matter which of the two options above you resonate with more, it's important to recognize that every choice you make is being driven by something; like who you hang out with, what college to go to, who to date, how you spend your time and where all your energy goes. You have a drive for everything, whether you know it or not. I want you to recognize this because you can have a drive, but it's not always in good ways or for good reasons.

Let's look at the highlighted verse for this chapter in Proverbs 31:

"She sets about her work vigorously

(this is her actively being driven);

her arms are strong for her tasks

(she has greater endurance).

She sees

(she has a vision here, vision plays a huge role to being driven)

that her trading is profitable,

(motivation),

and her lamp does not go out at night"

(Again, persistence, drive).

TWO KEY POINTS:

⊙ Her work is profitable.

⊙ Her lamp doesn't go out (this means that she is doing something sustainable. Not that sometimes she is driven, and sometimes she's not. This is a picture to show us this woman is 24/7 driven!)

Well, shoot. This makes me think of the C.S. Lewis quote a few pages back about how our faith is founded in something that is not affected by our mood. If you're motivated to go to the gym because you're in a go-getter mood, then as soon as your mood changes, you won't want to go to the gym. But if you go to the gym because you believe it's necessary to stay healthy and that's important to you, then you'll go every day!

The difference between these scenarios is the word "believe." What belief is driving you?

Some of the biggest things we must believe or have faith in is that God is the author or the story of the world. He loves us, and He is trustworthy. Challenge yourself to spend *daily* time in the Bible (His story), in prayer (love Him back) and seeking His will for your every moment (put your trust in Him). We must be connected to these truths so that action will be birthed out of these beliefs. Faith, belief, and connection with a God we cannot see or touch is cultivated in our steady pursuit of Him. Want to be more persuaded by the heart of God? Get to know Him better, ask Him his desire for this moment, tell Him about your day, and seek to share your heart with Him. The best way to start doing this is by spending quality time in His word daily, praying and seeking like stated above. But as your faith grows and your relationship with Him deepens, I'm certain that your relationship with the Lord will begin to look a lot more special and personal for you, thereby creating that drive within. If you have a best friend, don't you want to know everything about her? You learn what makes her angry and joyful about her past and her desires for the future. If you would seek after earthly relationships in this way, shouldn't we also seek after our relationship with God in the same way and even more?

Do you spend daily time reading the Bible or praying? Why or why not?

If we do not ground ourselves in these beliefs, we won't be driven to push forward in life, especially when things get hard! The drive is impossible without faith and belief, which ultimately is where vision comes from. Vision doesn't always mean literally seeing something physical, rather it means seeing the Man of Love standing before you, you see your King Jesus, and you believe all these truths stated above. Vision is having faith FOR what can be. And HE is the only one who can *persuade* us and give us *faith* in that.

Fear of the Lord plays a huge part in this. It makes us realize it's about more than our own happiness, but in fact, it's about the eternity of other people. That is enough reason to be driven to do something. Let this reality hit your heart and ask God what you can do to reach out to people. Dream big here. Think about other nations, think about Hollywood, think about New

York fashion week. I know people in all these places who are *driven* despite the hard times, and the perseverance it requires because they've been persuaded by the heart of God. They believed they found vision with purpose, and they ran hard.

One last piece of application before we close is for those of us that struggle with finding our vision (And believe me, girl, that's everyone at some point in their lives!) I believe our drive is found in our belief in God's "Him centered story." But what about the vision, where does that come from? While a lot of finding our vision is open to interpretation and between you and the Lord, if you are ever struggling, we can always find three key mandates for all believers in the Gospels.

The first two are found in Matthew 22.

"But when the Pharisees heard that he had silenced the Sadducees, they gathered together. And one of them, a lawyer, asked him a question to test him. "Teacher, which is the great commandment in the Law?" And he said to him, "You shall love the Lord your God with all your heart and with all your soul and with all your mind. This is the great and first commandment. And a second is like it: You shall love your neighbor as yourself. On these two commandments depend all the Law and the Prophets."

And the third is in Matthew 28.

"Go therefore and make disciples of all nations, baptizing them in the name of the father and of the son and of the Holy Spirit."

No matter where God calls you, when He calls you, whether you hear from Him or not, you can be assured He wants you to be spreading His Gospel while you love him and other people above all else. We will talk more about making disciples in the "Homemaker" chapter, but I just wanted to make sure I hit that in case you feel a bit lost! Remember, God calls us in seasons or assignments. Maybe he's called you into an assignment or mission, maybe he hasn't or maybe you're between assignments. Whatever your circumstances, love the Lord your God above all else, love other people, even strangers, and share his Gospel!

At the very least this is what we should be driven to do.

Group Questions

1. Do you spend daily time reading your Bible and praying? Why or why not? List some ways we can keep each other accountable for doing so.

2. Do you feel like you have a grasp on God's vision for this season of your life? If not, what do you think about the mandate to make disciples? (Again, we'll dive deeper into that in the Homemaker chapter, but let's get the conversation started!)

3. Describe a time you felt driven or motivated. What was driving you? How can you apply that to your spiritual life and personal disciplines?

Group Blessing

God, we thank you for being someone we can trust. Your steadfastness endures forever. We put our future in your hands. We trust you with all that we have. We give you our burdens and our worries. Take everything holding us back and fill us with a purpose and mission for you. Reveal to us your desire for our time, season and life. Be the wind in our sails and our driving force. Let us be driven by you, no matter the mood or the circumstances toward your goals and your vision.

Amen.

Forward Thinking

By Julienne Seely

Proverbs 31:21, 25

When it snows, she has no fear for her household;
for all of them are clothed in scarlet... she laughs without fear of the future.

Forward Thinking *(v) 1. Thinking about and planning for the future. (a) 1. Proactively showing leadership, courage and commitment, by concerning oneself with the future.*

God is the Author

As a little girl, I heard of God's wondrous creation and of His love for me. I thought He must be as nice as my Daddy. As a teen, I heard that He allowed the brutal sacrifice of His Son, and I thought He must not be entirely nice. And then, as a young adult, it was all put in perspective for me. I learned that my sin had necessitated this "nice Daddy's" sacrifice. Upon realizing this, I was deeply grateful and placed my whole trust in Him...or so I thought.

I gratefully accepted His free gift of eternal life... But I thought I knew exactly how He should fix life's challenges. I earnestly explained exactly what I hoped He would do to fix things. As I kept a prayer journal and invested myself in recording my requests and the results, I began to notice something interesting. My God took care of things I had not entrusted to Him. And He was resolving the situations I did pray about in ways I didn't suggest. He didn't seem to need my "instructions" at all!

When have you experienced God taking care of something you hadn't thought to pray for?

One of the things I love about living in the Midwest is the changing seasons--spring being my personal favorite. Surely, as the sun rises and sets, these seasons come and go, sometimes accompanied by unexpected storms. As demonstrated by the Proverbs 31 woman, a wise woman will have prepared her household to endure the temporary setbacks these storms can cause.

However, we are not always as well prepared for the emotional seasons we experience. We love the light-hearted times, but eventually, (and sometimes with no warning at all) a winter season will come for each of us. That winter can be identified by some kind of loss--of vision, spouse, parents, employment, innocence, confidence, hope. Such loss can come without warning, or it can be an inevitable outcome of a slow and painful process of decline, which is most unwelcome. So, how do we hold on? How do we face the future and see God's continued plan for our lives when it looks like everything is spinning out of control?

. . . .

"But Ruth said, "Do not urge me to leave you or to return from following you. For where you go I will go, and where you lodge I will lodge. Your people shall be my people, and your God my God. Where you die I will die, and there will I be buried. May the Lord *do so to me and more also if anything but death parts me from you."*

-Ruth 1:16-17

Consider the Bible's account of Ruth, who was married for ten years before her winter came, and she faced the loss of not only her husband but his brothers as well. Evidently, during those years, Ruth had learned from her husband to trust the God of Abraham. That shared faith gave her a new identity as a daughter of the King, and it prepared her to face widowhood with strength and dignity. When given a chance to return to her old life, she instead remained steadfast in the new one God had given her. He was the author of the story. She understood that there is more to life than what she could see at the moment.

When Ruth lost her husband and a majority of his family, the only family member left was her mother-in-law, Naomi. Choosing to stay with her and help provide for her, God continued to guide her to a new home and a new marriage. He also honored her faithfulness by allowing her to become a key person in the lineage of King David and eventually, the earthly lineage of the Messiah.

What guidance does that provide for us? Ruth continued to trust God and His plans for her even while she was experiencing grief and loss. As we learn to recognize His hand as He writes the story, both in the ordinary and difficult days, we are gradually building a trust relationship with Him that will prepare our hearts to face the stormiest of seasons.

The Bible history of Joseph (Genesis 37, 39-45) teaches us so much about how God's hand moves in the lives of His chosen vessels. In Joseph's life, everything God planned seemed diametrical to what Joseph had in mind. While he wanted to be elevated to greatness, God allowed him to be sold into slavery. Joseph wanted to advance during his service in Potiphar's house, but instead, God allowed him to be cast into prison. Joseph wanted to get out of prison, but God allowed him to stay there and be elevated as an overseer of other prisoners. And then, at the perfect time for God's purpose, Joseph was allowed to not only leave prison but also to be ranked in a position of high honor.

Has there been a time in your life when you had no idea what God was doing? Describe that time in your life:

He's an author! He is always working behind the scenes, and He is writing the story of your life. You might not know why He has you where He does, but He knows the plans He has for you. (Jeremiah 29:11) They will suit His divine purposes if only you *prayerfully give Him your permission to direct your steps down unknown paths.*

Recap this section in your own words. How can the truth "God is author" help us be forward thinking?

Personal Story

I see the same dynamic in my own life. I was married for 50 years, 8 months, 1 day and 20 hours. As my husband and I grew through those decades, we trusted the Lord during the blessed highs and the challenging lows. There is no way for me to know how things will be different in eternity because of what we did in those years. But I do know that I learned to trust

God's purposes daily, especially in allowing me to face the myriad challenges of my own personal development. Saying farewell to my parents' generation, one dear life at a time; occasionally setting aside my comfort and preferences in order to meet those of my family; supporting my husband through job loss and job challenges; facing my own personal failures; and giving birth to, and over time, releasing four precious children.

I knew I was living a blessed life, and I wanted it to continue undisturbed forever. However, as I learned to trust God in the many small details, He continued His work all around me, and I found myself prepared to face the harshest winter of my life.

My husband and I had been preparing for the soon arrival of our out-of-town family to celebrate Thanksgiving. First, we enjoyed a late, leisurely breakfast together, and then I went grocery shopping for the BIG feast just four days away. When I returned home, I was shocked to discover that he had died suddenly, quietly and alone after I left for the store. I knelt next to him and heartbroken tears flowed freely as I held his hand and thanked God for the many years we had shared. As I stayed alone with him for a while, praying and remembering, he grew colder, so I covered him carefully with a blanket and cushioned his head with a pillow. Finally, I reluctantly committed him to God's watch and care, and I began to call the family.

From that moment, feeling lost and desperately alone, I have been surprised to find myself "lifted on wings as eagles" (Isaiah 40:31), learning what each new day means and constantly being strengthened by my God's unfailing grace.

I have no idea why I was the one left here, and a big part of my grief process has been to accept God's plan in that regard. But as I've worked my way through each day (with some easier than others), my confidence has grown in a God who has not wandered at all from His eternal plan and I realize that He still has some use for me in His grand scheme of things. There is still work to do and like Jesus, I must be about my Father's business.

Don't expect your life to proceed without testing and know that sometimes those tests will break your heart. God will comfort your heart during those times, but He will also press forward in refining your heart. Seek God's guidance as you plunge into each new day. Be thankful for the days when it seems He is merely grooming and preparing you. Above all, look to Him to provide the strength and dignity to persevere on the days when you are under great pressure. Trust that God's plan for you is to profit and persevere you as He reaches His world through your life.

Application

Let's look at how you can trust God and live profitably for Him even when you don't understand what is happening. You can still proceed with making plans and moving forward but hold those plans lightly. Offer them up to Him and be ready to see how He might revise or redirect them. When those re-directions come, realize that you are witnessing His hand at work.

Do you regularly give God permission to disrupt your plans? Write about why or why not. If something is holding you back, pray about that.

For instance, you need to do your best in school or at work as preparation for your next step. But realize that your plans for college or the career that entices you may be replaced by something even better--something you may have never even considered. Maybe you have plans to be a missionary in another country, but God wants you to buy an apartment that would be the perfect location for hosting small groups and Bible studies! We should wholeheartedly pursue our passions with an open hand and a prayerful heart as we inquire from the Lord the direction, He would want us to walk in. Relax and join God in the adventure of finding out where each new day will take you. And do so with the confidence of one who knows that the Author of the story has penciled in some details you didn't anticipate.

I find it very easy to absorb God's blessings without expressing any gratitude for them. If this is true for you also, you might find it helpful to set aside a few minutes of prayer time each morning to ponder the ways you were blessed the previous day. Take time to write them down along with their dates and thank the Lord for them.

As you inevitably also notice those things which are "awry" in your life, why not also write those down along with their dates? Take time to commit those issues to God telling Him that you are placing them in His hands and that you trust Him to work His good will in them. God always answers, but He doesn't always answer, "Yes." His timing may allow you to invest yourself in exercising your trust daily for weeks--or even years--as He moves to resolve all the intricate details of the issue you've placed before Him. At those times, He says, "Wait. Trust Me in this."

Sometimes He replies with a resounding and disappointing, "No, my child!"

I am reminded of the little boy who begged his father to give him a B-B gun. When his dad did so, the little boy went right out and shot a little bird singing on the fence in their yard. Then the little boy asked dad for a higher-powered weapon, and his dad wisely replied, "No, son. If I did what you're asking, you'd kill yourself with it!" Sometimes we are simply not prepared to use a blessing well. If that's the case, just like that little boy, we can trust our heavenly Father to know when we are ready.

Prayerfully commit to the Lord some circumstances, plans or relationships in your life right now.

It has also been my experience that sometimes, God says, "You're not thinking big enough. Just take a look at what I'm going to do for you!" And then He shows Himself mighty on my behalf in such a way that I'm left speechless.

There are times you trust God in an issue, but you don't really know all the details of the matter. Or perhaps, you don't know all the issues that are also going to be resolved along with the one that concerns you. But God sees the big picture and He may be busy at work "knocking down dominoes" in a careful pattern that leads straight to the heart of the matter that concerns you. Have patience.

Our prayer life is not to be focused only on ourselves. We have a great opportunity and responsibility to pray on behalf of the needs of others too. Over the years, the nature of my intercessory prayer life, or praying on behalf of others has changed. I used to ask, "Do you have something you want me to pray about?" But now I ask, "How can I be trusting God on your behalf?" And then I carry those needs to the cross, lay them down at the feet of the One who I trust completely, and leave them there with confidence.

When you have an active, living trust in God's perfect power and intent, your attitude tends to rub off on others. Your family, work associates, fellow believers, and friends would listen to you as they see you living your life in optimistic hope. Faith is contagious, and it is strengthening. Have you ever gotten a "spiritual high" ready to go out into the world and be the best possible Christian you can be after an epic spiritual experience like a camp or worship concert or Christian conference? Why not live every day like that? In fellowship with fellow believers, live out the will of the Lord with a contagious zeal.

One of my ancestors traveled to the state of Washington in a covered wagon. He found his way by following a trail that had been traveled by so many others. The wheel tracks of those who had passed through that road carved a pathway in the stone. We create such a guide for succeeding generations as we consistently and persistently make our requests known unto God, and He grants us a peace that passes all understanding. (Philippians 4:7) What better legacy could we create as we, like the Proverbs woman, laugh without fear for the future because we have committed our lives to the great story our trustworthy Lord is writing?

So overall, we can see that being an active prayer warrior is the best way to place our future in God's hands. But if you'd like a practical application as well, we can see that the Proverbs 31 Woman "had no fear for her household; for all of them are clothed in scarlet." She not only knew that God was the author and trusted her future to Him, but she also made clothing for all of her household. Nowadays, whether your household is just you or if you have others you care for, thinking ahead is always important. Depending on your season of life, this could look like learning to do your own taxes, saving money, taking care of your car, researching exactly what you want to do with your future (career, motherhood, entrepreneur, etc.) and preparing thusly.

But regardless, always remember that God is the author of the world! He is the one who calls you by name, whose will is good and whose might is limitless. What's unbelievable is how that same God cares about your future and wants you to trust Him with it.

. . . .

"Ask, and it will be given to you; seek, and you will find; knock, and it will be opened to you. For everyone who asks receives, and the one who seeks finds, and to the one who knocks it will be opened. Or which one of you, if his son asks him for bread, will give him a stone? Or if he asks for a fish, will give him a serpent? If you then, who are evil, know how to give good gifts to your children, how much more will your Father who is in heaven give good things to those who ask him!"

-Matthew 7:7-11

How can you be forward-thinking? By placing your needs, desires, thoughts and fears in His hands, combined with wise stewardship over this life, He has given you on earth.

Group Questions

1. What does your prayer life look like? What are some of the biggest things you struggle with in prayer?

2. When you experience fear of the future, how do you handle it?

3. Have you given God authority over your life and future? Do you trust Him with your future?

4. If you believed that God was the author, at a 10/10...how do you think it would impact your life?

Group Blessing

Lord, thank you for being the great author. You write my story and the story of the world, but most importantly, your story, with excellence, forethought, and power. You know when I lie down and when I get up. You see beyond human limitation and your hand is in everything. We give you permission over our lives, our future, our hopes and dreams. Please allow your will to be done through our lives. Lord, please, send us in your name and give us assignments. We want to be active for your Kingdom and in pursuit of truth and love in all we do.

Amen.

Homemaker

By Kelsey Pryor

Proverbs 31:11-13, 22, 27

Her husband has full confidence in her and lacks nothing of value. She brings him good, not harm, all the days of her life. She selects wool and flax and works with eager hands. She makes coverings for her bed; she is clothed in fine linen and purple. She watches over the affairs of her household and does not eat the bread of idleness.

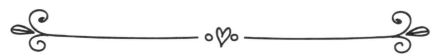

Homemaker *(n) 1. a person who manages a home.*

Jesus is the Bridegroom

Right off the bat, I'm going to be honest. I'm 19, I'm not a wife, I don't own a house, and I don't own a field.... Just throwing that out there.

Now, for the sake of this chapter, I'm going to assume you don't own a house or field or have a husband, just like me! Knowing this, how in the world are we supposed to apply these verses of Proverbs 31 to our lives?

In this chapter, we will look at the three things, we as single people, might see as barriers in this verse. They include the lack of a husband, the lack of property, and the lack of a household. Also, I'm going to show you that while we might lack those physical traits, these verses most certainly still apply to us right now.

The first barrier is the lack of a husband. I know if you're like me, you're probably lamenting this crucial detail. But all longings for a spouse aside, it's true. You are not a wife and so your husband couldn't possibly "have full confidence in you," and you can't "bring him good all the days of his life," right?

Wrong.

Friends, there is a bigger story at play. God has a love story for you, and that is far grander than any love story between you and a man on earth. The love story we are all longing and hoping for deep down isn't for a man on earth, but with Jesus. Jesus is your bridegroom. In fact, marriage on earth only exists to represent the marriage of Jesus with His people! It's simply a metaphor.

What does this stir up for you? Have you ever thought of Jesus as your groom?

I know a common cliché about Christian girls is that they're "dating Jesus," and I hate clichés. So, we aren't even going to talk about it like this. What I'm talking about is a betrothal that has been planned since way before you were born. I'm talking about the most epic wedding that is yet to take place. A bringing together of you, the bride, dressed in white to your husband, the Prince of Peace. It is coming, rejoice!

"Then the disciples of John came to him, saying, "Why do we and the Pharisees fast,[c] but your disciples do not fast?" And Jesus said to them, "Can the wedding guests mourn as long as the bridegroom is with them? The days will come when the bridegroom is taken away from them, and then they will fast."

–Matthew 9:14-15

We see in Matthew, where Jesus refers to Himself as the Bridegroom. Then, after the resurrection, His saying came true, and He was taken away. We are currently in a state of waiting for our bridegroom to come back.

In the cultural practice of betrothal, a woman is promised to a man from a young age. When the time of their marriage is coming close, the groom will go away to prepare a home for his bride. Sometimes this meant actually building her a house! So, the bride makes all the preparations for the wedding to happen at any given moment because she doesn't know when her groom will arrive. Then one day, the groom would come back to his bride, sometimes actually riding on a white horse! Once they get married, he takes her back to the home he has been preparing. (If you want a resource on this, watch the documentary "Betrothed" on www.heaventv7.com. It's about a modern- day couple reigniting this ancient practice, and it's so beautiful!)

So, as we wait for Jesus to come back, you can say we are like the bride who must be ready at any moment for her beloved to return. Meanwhile, we can rest knowing he is preparing a home for us with many rooms. (John 14:2)

What are some things a bride can do in preparation for her husband that we can do in preparation for Jesus' return?

"Let us rejoice and exult and give him the glory, for the marriage of the Lamb has come, and his Bride has made herself ready,"

– Revelation 19:7

Then in Revelation, a book of prophecy that describes the end-times tells us that there will be a giant wedding feast, and Jesus, the Lamb, will come back for His bride! All throughout the New Testament, the Church of Jesus that is His disciples and followers are referred to as the Bride of Christ. If you are a disciple of Jesus and a follower of the one true God, then you are a part of that church and you are His bride waiting for His return!

So, in this Proverbs 31 verse, when it talks about her husband having confidence in her and she brings him good, not harm... let's envision Jesus as our husband. What would it look like for Jesus to look down on us as He prepares our wedding and thinks, "Wow, I have full confidence in her." Don't be put off by the word "husband," either. Earthly wives and husbands are merely actors in a drama, characters in a story, not the real thing! As a single, you have the opportunity to take full advantage of the *real thing* and take on the identity as Jesus' bride!

How might we act differently when our motivation is to bring Jesus good and not harm?

We'll get into how to practically apply that in a second. For now, let's move onto our 2nd tension for singles with this verse, which is a lack of property, whether it's a house, a field or expensive belongings. The Proverbs 31 woman is described as gathering wool and flax, making her own bedding and being clothed in fine linen. I don't know about you, but I shop at the thrift store and I don't think I've ever touched actual wool and flax straight out of a field... (But I do make my own quilts. I'll admit to that.)

ANYWAYS, how is this image of an ideal woman supposed to apply today? Even those of you reading this who might be married or own a home would find this concept kind of outdated. But as we have done with most chapters in this book, we must look at the intention, the heart, and the motivation behind the verses, not necessarily the actual application of them. The characteristic we see here is that she is a hard worker and hospitable. We've talked about being hardworking in another chapter, so let's focus on the hospitable part.

Why should we be hospitable? Well, similarly to the chapter on generosity, the only reason you own anything at all is because God gave it to you. He is the provider of everything. If you enter into the mindset of "I was given this, so I should have no problem giving it to someone else," it puts you in a posture of generosity and hospitality. When someone enters your property, be it a car, a room, a house, an apartment, or whatever, are they physically or emotionally or spiritually at home? Do they feel like Jesus lives there? Do they feel like it is a refuge or a place of love or an intentionally crafted space?

List some things you own or are a steward of.

This can be hard for a lot of people, including me. But I just have to remind myself to tell the Lord, "Thank you for giving me this couch. How can I use it to serve you? Thank you for giving me this blanket. How can I use it to serve you? Thank you for giving me this car. How can I use it to serve you?"

Our last tension for singles with this Proverbs 31 passage is our lack of household or family. What do I mean by household? Do you have to own a house? Nope. In the passage, I think the household refers to the husband, children and servants of the woman. But because we don't have those things, we are going to look at it as disciples.

How would you define "disciple?"

Now the wedding analogy through the New Testament is used to describe the bringing together of Jesus the groom with his bride the Church, right? Well another way it's illustrated here in Matthew is like God the father, throwing a wedding feast for his son! The father wants lots of guests to be there to celebrate. Let's take a look at this parable from Jesus:

. . . .

"Jesus spoke to them again in parables, saying: "The kingdom of heaven is like a king who prepared a wedding banquet for his son. He sent his servants to those who had been invited to the banquet to tell them to come, but they refused to come.

"Then he sent some more servants and said, 'Tell those who have been invited that I have prepared my dinner: My oxen and fattened cattle have been butchered, and everything is ready. Come to the wedding banquet.'

"But they paid no attention and went off—one to his field, another to his business. The rest seized his servants, mistreated them and killed them. The king was enraged. He sent his army and destroyed those murderers and burned their city.

"Then he said to his servants, 'The wedding banquet is ready, but those I invited did not deserve to come. So go to the street corners and invite to the banquet anyone you find.' So the servants went out into the streets and gathered all the people they could find, the bad as well as the good, and the wedding hall was filled with guests.

"But when the king came in to see the guests, he noticed a man there who was not wearing wedding clothes. He asked, 'How did you get in here without wedding clothes, friend?' The man was speechless. "Then the king told the attendants, 'Tie him hand and foot, and throw him outside, into the darkness, where there will be weeping and gnashing of teeth.' "For many are invited, but few are chosen."

-Matthew 22:1-14

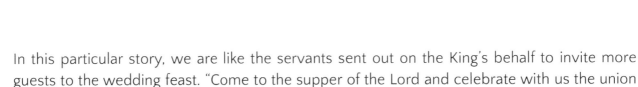

In this particular story, we are like the servants sent out on the King's behalf to invite more guests to the wedding feast. "Come to the supper of the Lord and celebrate with us the union of the Church with her groom Jesus!" It is one of our biggest callings as disciples to go and make more disciples (Matthew 28:16-20). This wedding is going to be the biggest celebration in history, a union of all believers with their husband Jesus! We want as many people to be apart of that as possible!

When someone is married and has kids, their children are like their disciples. But for us who have no children, our disciples are like our children and so like our household. Paul, one of the most famous singles of the Bible, used this verbiage all the time! In1 Timothy 1:2 he calls Timothy, his disciple and his son in the faith. All throughout 1 Corinthians, he calls the church of Corinth his brothers and sisters!

The verses below offer an even more specific example:

"Sing, barren woman,
you who never bore a child;
burst into song, shout for joy, you who were never in labor;
because more are the children of the desolate woman
than of her who has a husband,"
says the Lord. For your Maker is your husband,
the Lord Almighty is his name; the Holy One
of Israel is your Redeemer,
he is called the God of all the earth." [b]

-Isaiah 54:1, 5

The woman with no husband, and who was never pregnant has more children! Why? Because discipleship is foretold, and she has the unique opportunity to make disciples endlessly without restraints or earthly confines by a family. Don't get me wrong. Marriage is wonderful. It is a blessing and married women can also make disciples! But the gift of the single is her flexibility, her ability to be unbound with the purpose to further the Kingdom of the Lord and multiply by making disciples.

How might our lives look if we viewed our disciples as our mission, descendants and blessing?

So, with these three elements working together, our husband and partner, Jesus, hospitality with our few belongings and property, and the people of our household being those we disciple.... It has all the makings of a homemaker.

Recap this section in your own words. How can the God Truth of "Jesus is our Bridegroom" help us be Homemakers?

Personal Story

Here's an interesting tidbit... I wasn't going to add a Personal Story section to this chapter, but some events have occurred in my life just as I'm writing this book that I have to share!

When it comes to Jesus being my groom... I started to believe it in a new way recently because there was a lie, I consistently believed about myself, which I believe lots of women struggle with; I'm not enough. This occurs mostly in relationships! Have you ever felt that? So, I was journal praying about it the other day. I did this exercise where you'd write down your most honest prayer to God, get all of it out there, and then list the lies you are believing. Then, write a note to yourself from God's perspective. What does He say about you? So, I wrote down the lie that I'm not enough and then what I wrote for my note from God surprised me! I wrote, "Kelsey, you aren't enough... apart from me. I'm your source, your sustainer, your everlasting. The closer you get to me, the more "enough" you are. In God's sight, you are precious." I loved this because out of my own strength, it's true! I can't possibly do enough to become "enough." I can't fulfill anyone's needs, and no one can fulfill my needs. But the closer we get to Jesus, we are fulfilled in Him and He is enough for us and that's all that matters! If the Lord hasn't given you a husband yet, that means you don't need one! Read Psalm 23, "The LORD is my shepherd. I lack nothing!"

Okay, so when it comes to hospitality... I recently redesigned my bedroom. It was super fun! But my intention behind it was to create a place people would want to be. I wanted people to feel comfortable physically and welcomed and spiritually safe and secure. My heart for this space is that I can host young women to stay with me or just come over whenever they want and be loved on and also a place to host Bible studies or worship times, which I've done, and it's been so special!

And lastly, for disciple-making, my journey on this has been quite interesting. Up until a few weeks ago, my approach to disciple-making was quite laid back and high thought, low action. I wanted to wait until the right people would be involved with me until my room was ready to host, and until I had time in my schedule to make a consistent time for building into young ladies. Now I realize that doesn't completely align with scripture. Sure, you should be thoughtful about this kind of thing, but the first step is always to take the first step! You're never going to have it all figured out so you might as well start now. What did the disciples do when someone decided to follow Jesus? They baptized them RIGHT THEN! How wild is that?? So recently, I had someone challenge my evangelism and it really shook my views and the way I think about everything! Every interaction with someone the person standing in line next to you, the homeless person who stops you and asks for money, your cashier, etc. should be a used opportunity to say Jesus' name! Tell someone the good news today! But don't get me wrong, I still want to strategize it. I've started a super basic, simple Bible Study on the Gospels at my house on Sunday afternoons, so if someone I share the gospel with wants to go deeper, I have something I can invite them to! Then any girl in my life that wants me to disciple them or are looking for people to disciple them can also come and find the right person or learn something about Jesus or be held accountable. I haven't been using this strategy for long, but I know lots of people that have, and it's been a huge success for them. So, I hope to be able to continually share my discoveries, findings, wins and fails with you all on our website or our social media!

Application

Okay, so we have looked at what it looked like for me, now let's figure out how it could possibly be for you!

Let's first look at how to apply the belief that Jesus is our bridegroom. This can be hard for a lot of people, myself included.

Is this hard for you to believe? If so, why?

Maybe you have a wounding from a past relationship, or you're in a great relationship and don't want to think about Jesus replacing your significant other, or maybe it just sounds downright weird! All of these are valid points. I think what helps me when I struggle with this concept is remembering that everything on this earth is merely a representation of a greater story God has set in motion.

We need food to remind ourselves that earthly things can only sustain us for a short amount of time, but God can sustain us forever. Baptism represents us dying to ourselves and being resurrected in Jesus and giving our lives to Him. Parents and children represent our relationship with God the Father, while marriage represents our relationship with Jesus, our groom.

If we are able to look at it that way, we can know that it's totally okay and even good to still have earthly relationships and significant others because it's something God has set into motion with the two very first people He created! However, we need a continual reminder that the earthly relationship between you and your spouse is sacred and special but not sustaining and not everlasting. Jesus is our true partner. He is the one we are supposed to make Lord over our lives (Romans 10:9). He is the one we can always turn to, who always saves us and knows what's best for us.

He will never cease to love you.

Rewrite the above sentence 3 times.

Now, what about applying hospitality? We've talked about how it pertains to Proverbs 31 and why it's important, but how are we supposed to be hospitable? Some of you might have a house or apartment, but most of you might only have a room at your parent's house or a dorm room. Then, how are you supposed to be hospitable?

Working hard to make whatever property we do have hospitable to others is something I think we can all strive for. Let's say all you own is a car, that's great! Offer to give people rides, keep it clean, and maybe even lend it out when your friend is in need. If you have your own apartment, it doesn't matter if you don't have fancy furniture or gorgeous decor, invite people into it, have food to offer them, and a place they can sit and talk. If you still live at home and all you have is a small bedroom, what do you do with it? How do you present the small bit of property you have? If your friend needs a night away from home, do you offer them your bed? Do you use the space to cultivate conversation around Jesus and make it a place of encouragement and uplifting?

List 3 ways you can be hospitable with what you own or steward.

Hospitality can look different for all kinds of people. So, I'm not going to tell you exactly what to do with your stuff, but I will tell you not to be stingy. Always look for ways to make it a place of refuge and comfort to your friends or even strangers or mild acquaintances. Tell the Lord, "Thank you for giving me this bed. How can I use it to serve you? Thank you for giving me a shower with soap. How can I use it to serve you?"

And finally, how can we apply the belief that our disciples are like our spiritual children? The concept of making disciples is one the Bible makes clear we are to actively do, but it can also be hard to figure out how to do it practically.

"And Jesus came and said to them, "All authority in heaven and on earth has been given to me. Go therefore and make disciples of all nations, baptizing them in the name of the Father and of the Son and of the Holy Spirit, teaching them to observe all that I have commanded you. And behold, I am with you always, to the end of the age."

– Matthew 28:18-20

I want to encourage the young and unmarried among you: You are uniquely gifted for this role. Married people have the amazing ability to also make disciples and bring them into their homes and families. However, the presence of a family can sometimes make them less flexible. For those who are not married, you have the beautiful gift of flexibility to go where the Lord calls you and initiate conversations and interactions in the most unlikely of places.

We have 2 main examples of disciple-making singles in the Bible: Jesus and Paul. They both went about their ministry very differently but very effectively. Jesus made disciples everywhere He went, but He chose 12 of them to specifically invest in and to follow Him everywhere He went. In our chapter about generosity, Addie talked about how her youth ministry leader made a huge impact on her just by letting her spend a lot of time with her! She let her see the ins and outs of her life, the messy and the tidy.

Paul traveled from church to church to preach the gospel, and along the way, he made many disciples like Titus and Timothy, who then went on and did the same thing he did. This is a great example of multiplication. You might just be one person, but if you make 5 disciples and those disciples go ahead and make 5 disciples each and so on... you could affect hundreds of people just by your investment in 5! You could have 100 "great- grandchildren" before you even get married!

Is there a non-believer in your life that you could tell the Gospel to? List a few ways you can tell her about Jesus and show her the hope you have! If you aren't in a situation where you regularly encounter non-Christians, I suggest journaling or praying about that and asking the Lord how you can insert yourself in a situation where you weekly encounter non-believers. Use that interaction to share the Gospel with them.

Is there a believer in your life that you could be there for and encourage in the Word? List a few ways you can love, support, encourage and show her Jesus!

So again, I can't tell you the exact method that works with your life because that's between you and the Lord, however, I can give you examples and encourage you to look for opportunities around you to invest in, reach out to, and even just pray for those around you.

Some awesome ministries with the content on discipleship or resources that I love are:

- https://1kh.org *(content on how to make disciples)*

- https://wellwateredwomen.com *(resources for scripture study)*

- And of course, our own website https://withstrengthanddignity.com *(community, resources, content all pertaining to discipleship)*

I hope you are encouraged as you realize that you already have all the makings of a Proverbs 31 homemaker! Communicate with your groom, give him control of the wheel of your life so you can live your life in such a way that gives him "full confidence" in you. Take whatever belongings or property you have and use it to show unquestionable hospitality to those around you. Steadfastly, seek ways to share the gospel, train up and lead disciples, and watch your household grow!

Group Questions

1. Do you have any blocks when it comes to thinking of Jesus as the groom of the Church and thus your groom? Why?

2. Share how you intend to be generously hospitable with the resources you steward!

3. Do you have regular times in your week where you share the Gospel, disciple someone or are being discipled? If not, discuss what are some practical steps might be to move toward those!

Group Blessing

Jesus, thank you for being our rescuer. Thank you for being our Savior and thank you for choosing us as your bride! We desire to please you in all that we do, and for you to call us a faithful bride worthy of your confidence. Please, help us steward our resources well and be generously hospitable to everyone we meet. As we do our best to live out our great commission of disciple-making, direct our path and bring people into our lives that you want us to pursue. Give us the boldness it takes to share the gospel and infuse us with the zeal to bring about your Kingdom on earth as it is in heaven.

Amen.

Respected and Noble

By Alyssa Bethke

Proverbs 31: 23, 28-29, 31

Her husband is respected at the city gate, where he takes his seat among the elders of the land. Her children arise and call her blessed; her husband also, and he praises her: "Many women do noble things, but you surpass them all." Honor her for all that her hands have done, and let her works bring her praise at the city gate.

Noble *(a) 1. Having or showing fine personal qualities or high moral principles and ideals. righteous, virtuous, good, honorable, honest, upright, upstanding, decent, worthy, noble*

Respect *(v) 1. Having due regard for the feelings, wishes, rights, or traditions of. 2. Admire (someone or something) deeply, as a result of their abilities, qualities, or achievements.*

God is our King

Throughout the Bible, there is a story being told; it's not just tons of verses about how to live, or even who we are and how God has saved us. But rather it tells a beautiful, dramatic, epic story of God who created the world and all of us out of His great love. A story of how we chose to go our own way and pushed God out of the picture, but how He relentlessly is after His children, His bride, and His church. Throughout Scripture, God is described as many things; some being our Creator, our Father, our Savior, our Friend, and King.

Living in America, we don't get the full impact of what it means that God is King. We see glimpses of it from England where we see the Royal Family, in movies, or in books that talk about royalty. We read about it in history, but we simply don't operate in the U.S. with kings and queens, dukes and duchesses, and lords. So, we most likely don't tend to think much of God as King, except that we acknowledge He reigns and has the final say. The book of Revelation peels back the curtain a bit and gives us a vision of God as King.

"At once I was in the Spirit, and behold, a throne stood in heaven, with one seated on the throne. And he who sat there had the appearance of jasper and carnelian, and around the throne was a rainbow that had the appearance of an emerald."

-Revelation 4:2-3

John (the author and one who is having this vision) then goes on to tell about the elders and four living creatures that are around God's throne. They worship Him day and night! Here's what he said about them,

"And whenever the living creatures give glory and honor and thanks to him who is seated on the throne, who lives forever and ever, the twenty-four elders fall down before him who is seated on the throne and worship him who lives forever and ever. They cast

their crowns before the throne saying, "worthy are you, our Lord and God, to receive glory and honor and power, for you created all things, and by your will they existed and were created"

-Revelation 4:9-11

God as King is not just God reigning and ruling, or God wearing a crown and demanding for us to obey Him. Rather, He's seated in heaven, in all His glory and holiness, and when we are finally with Him, we won't be able to help but fall to our faces in total adoration, praise and awe of Him. I'm sure I'll cry buckets of tears because finally, I will be in His full presence and will FEEL His rich and deep love and be in complete awe of who He is. That HE, the God of the Universe who is over all and in all and through all- the God who has held the world, and me in His hands- all my circumstances- and my story. The God who held me in my pain and the God who danced with me in my joy- He is the Almighty King.

What does "Almighty King" mean to you? What would your life look like if you lived as a subject of such a King?

And the crazy thing is, we not only are loved by the King, we not only have the attention of the King, but we are His daughters. We're in the family. We have a beautiful inheritance. We are His. We are part of the royal family.

"He shall cry to me, 'You are my Father, my God, and the Rock of my salvation.'"

-Psalm 89:26

"Father of the fatherless and protector of widows is God in his holy habitation."

-Psalm 68:5

Having the King as your Dad is a whole lot different than just being a bystander. We are welcomed into the inner circle. We are welcomed to run fully to Him and find our security in Him.

And because God is king and we are His daughters, we are also given great worth and responsibility. We are called to be noble and act with respect and honor. However, this isn't something we have to muster, or we'll be kicked out of the family if we mess up. Rather, it's a way of life that is an overflow of who we are. We live in a certain way because we know we are His, given such great worth and value.

Write: "I am called to be noble and act with respect and honor."

Recap this section in your own words. How can the truth "God is King" help us be respected and noble?

Personal Story

Growing up, we had these 8x5 brown signs hanging up by our beds had our names and their meanings. "Alyssa: noble, honorable," I remember looking at this sign all the time and memorizing it, yet I didn't fully understand what noble or honorable meant in my little 8-year-old heart.

And if I'm honest, I didn't fully understand its meaning until recently.

My parents both loved the Lord deeply, and growing up, they taught me all about Jesus. We went to church regularly, and they faithfully walked life with me, always pointing me to Jesus. I gave my life to Him, asking Him to be my Savior when I was 7, right after my Sunday school teacher told us about Jesus' death and resurrection with her felt board.

But it wasn't until I was 15 that I really started to walk with Him, and I understood that being a Christian isn't just about doing the right thing or going to church, but about a relationship with Him, that transforms everything. My heart started to long for Him, to know Him, to spend time with Him, to enter into His beautiful adventure that He had for me and to be a part of bringing his kingdom to earth. I loved the Lord with all my heart and longed for others to know Him too. I was a leader in the youth group, on the leadership team and worship team. Even in college, I was a Resident Assistant and led girl's Bible studies and mission trips.

But somehow, along the way, my thinking got askew and deep down, I believed that I had to earn God's love. I would never have said that out loud or even answered "yes" to that if someone asked me point-blank. But deep down in my heart, how I lived my life showed that to be true. I feared that if I missed reading my Bible that day, somehow, God would love me less or be disappointed in me. I feared that if I missed a Bible study that people would think I wasn't truly committed or godly enough. I feared that if I was truly vulnerable with what I actually thought about- my fears, worries, deep-unmet- desires, questions, and unchecked sins-that people wouldn't respect me or would question my walk with the Lord, or even worse, God would be upset with me. I wasn't living in true freedom, and it all started with this wrong belief.

Do you struggle with believing this? Describe.

And it's crazy to me because I knew this wasn't true. I knew the right answer- God's love is unconditional. He loves me like crazy, but I didn't fully believe it. I believed I had to earn God's love or rather, I had it, but it could always change or diminish based on what I did or didn't do. I knew I was His but didn't believe that I had worth because of what He did. I thought I gained worth by what I did or didn't do. When it comes to nobility, I did live a noble life. I did the right things, always had high moral principles and ideals, and cannot lie if my life depended on it! But my motives were not always pure. I lived a noble life out of fear instead of out of the overflow

of God's great love for me. I lived out of obligation instead of out of great joy and who He said I was. And because of that, oftentimes, I was judgmental of others in my heart and not gracious with them or myself. I held myself to such a high standard that it left no room for God's grace to flow in or out. Also, I held others to high standards, and it is evident in my life that I actually set high expectations on them that they couldn't meet.

I longed to be respected and still do. I want to be known as someone worth admiring and one who can be looked up to for people to seek my wisdom or thoughts. I want to be known as someone who is smart and wise. It's not wrong to want to be respected, but our motive should be to please God in the inner places of our hearts, not for others to notice us. We should live respectable or noble or do the right thing because we are His daughters; that's simply who we are. We long to live in the light and walk godly lives because we are women of God, not just because we want to be praised, noticed, or admired. It's so easy to long to be noticed. Hoping so-and-so sees me do this, or talk to this person, or say this great thing. Hoping my friends, family and people I looked up to noticed my accomplishments. However, in this era with social media, isn't this an easy trap to fall into? We sometimes gather our value based on how many followers we have or how many likes or comments we receive from a post.

But the person who tells us we are respectable and noble isn't our followers or our friends... it's our King! The Almighty King seated in Heaven's heights, on a mighty throne with the ultimate authority in heaven and earth... tells us we are noble. We are His, and so we are worthy of respect.

Do you believe you are His? Explain.

Application

Even with a good motive, we desperately need Jesus to live out being respectable and believing we are noble. We need Him. We are weak and don't often know what to do. We also tend to not see what's best, don't always choose the right thing or the respectable thing. Or we may choose the right thing and be ridiculed by it from our friends or coworkers! So, we know the source of our respectability and nobility comes from the identity Christ gives us in Him. But that doesn't mean we can just sit around on the couch, crunching on potato chips every night, glued to a screen and say, "Hey, I'm respectable because God says I am!" He also expects us to put actions to that identity and live a life like Christ did!

. . . .

"A good name is to be chosen rather than great riches, and favor is better than silver or gold."

-Proverbs 22:1

Here, we see that Proverbs tells us a good reputation is to be desired, and the reputation we should desire is based on our character rather than our image. We want a character that produces respect from others. So, how do we do that? How do we act in such a way that others can't help but respect us? How do we reflect the nobility we have inherited as ambassadors of The King?

Well, first of all, being respected (or respectable) is more of a characteristic, while being noble is more of an identity. So, the application for the two of these are a bit different. Believing you are noble might lead you to act more respectable or acting respectable might make it easier for you to accept your identity as nobility. Whichever way, they go hand in hand!

Think about the way royalty grows up; in a castle, with subjects and servants, their parents being the King and Queen... everywhere around them, they are told that they are royal. It's spoken over them, assumed of them, and called out of them. They are inherently aware of their position, and a good Prince or Princess will see it calls for a life of respectability. All they need to do is receive that identity. The same goes for you!

Meanwhile, it's a little harder since you aren't constantly reminded by your castle and royal parents that you are noble! But it's still the same. All you need to do is receive the identity of nobility. And that's all I can say for you because the rest is between you and your father, the King!

Next, why should you desire to be respectable? Or what does that even mean?

"As a prisoner for the Lord, then, I urge you to live a life worthy of the calling you have received."

- Ephesians 4:1

"So that you may live a life worthy of the Lord and please him in every way: bearing fruit in every good work, growing in the knowledge of God,"

- Colossians 1:10

You have been called as a daughter of the King, a princess, which makes you noble! These verses state that it is wise to live life according to the calling or purpose or identity God has placed on you. So, here are a few tips for being respectable:

1.

Live and speak with integrity. This means: speak the truth, don't be a hypocrite, have strong morals and walk in uprightness.

"Whoever walks in integrity walks securely, but he who makes his ways crooked will be found out."

-Proverbs 10:9

Rewrite this verse.

"Fine speech is not becoming to a fool; still less is false speech to a prince."

-Proverbs 17:7

Write what it means to be full of integrity and how you might do this.

2.

Serve with radical love. Always put others before yourself. Think of yourself last. Have compassion on the weak and have grace on those in need.

"Do nothing from selfish ambition or conceit, but in humility count others more significant than yourselves."

-Philippians 2:3

Rewrite this verse.

"[E]ven as the Son of Man came not to be served but to serve, and to give his life as a ransom for many."

- Matthew 20:28

Write what it means to serve with radical love and how you might do this.

3.

Live with ambitious humility. Seek success without pride.
Desire to do a job well done and then give God the glory.

"One's pride will bring him low, but he who is lowly in spirit will obtain honor."

-Proverbs 29:23

Rewrite this verse.

Write what it means to live with ambitious humility and how you might do this.

4.

Desire to learn. Seek knowledge and practice wisdom. Put your knowledge
into practice. Spend your time in a worthwhile pursuit of the truth.

"Let the wise hear and increase in learning, and the one who understands obtain guidance."

-Proverbs 1:5

Rewrite this verse.

Write what it means to desire to learn and how you might do this.

Now what do you think we should do when either we fall short or other people fall short? What are we supposed to do when someone doesn't act in a respectable way? Do they forfeit their right to be respected? Not necessarily. Let's think all the way back to the chapter on Valuable & Worthy, when Kelsey talked about how we are all image bearers of God. Remember how C.S. Lewis was particularly hit by this phenomena and decided to intentionally treat everyone he encountered as an image bearer of God? This should always hold true, no matter what a person's actions are. A person is worthy of love and should be seen as a valuable person with worth, merely because of who their Creator is! Because of this, even when it's hard and a persons actions or leadership or skills might seem disrespectable... we should continually strive to treat them as Jesus would, despite their actions!

Girl, just remember that you are an ambassador for Jesus- because you want to make Him look so glorious and to love His children like He loves them, and to be His great light that points to Him, not you. You are noble because you're a daughter of the Good and Mighty King. You are respected because He created you and gave you all your worth. He has given you gifts and strengths, and you will do amazing things because you're His, and you are created for His good works.

You are royalty. You are respectable because you're His.

Group Questions

1. Do you believe you are noble? If not, what is holding you back?

2. Did any of the above applications for being respectable sound strange or foreign to you? Did any of them seem like the most difficult to live out?

3. As you think about being an ambassador on behalf of the King, what does that stir up for you? Does it fill you with purpose or anxiety?

Group Blessing

Almighty King, we are so honored that you have chosen us to carry out your will as ambassadors and carriers of your name. Thank you for trusting us and calling us into your inner circle. We pray you help us believe the identity that we are nobility, that we are not only ambassadors but daughters of the King and thus royal. With that identity, we want to live a life worthy of the calling you have bestowed upon us with a respectable honor. Fill us with the desire and strength to go about our days in a respectable manner, holding our heads up high, bearing your insignia.

Amen.

Strength and Dignity

By Kelsey Pryor

Proverbs 31:25

She is clothed in strength and dignity...

Strength *(n) 1. A quiet confidence in the midst of the unknown. 2. the emotional or mental qualities necessary in dealing with situations or events that are distressing or difficult.*

Dignity *(n) 1. The full awareness of your worth, and the resolve to protect and profess it. 2. the state or quality of being worthy of honor or respect; self-respect.*

God is Our Father

Hopefully, you just read "Respected and Noble" and learned about how God is King. I will be expanding on that a lot in this chapter but will be adding another aspect, which stresses that God is also our *Father*. We'll talk a bit about that and then how that applies to us being strong and dignified.

"Who is this King of glory? The LORD of hosts, He is the King of glory!"

-Psalm 24:10

"See what kind of love the Father has given to us, that we should be called children of God;"

-1 John 3:1

If God is a King and we are His children, that kind of makes us princesses, right? And I don't mean princesses like our favorite Disney character... I mean princess like the King's daughter who is being trained how to rule. Not the damsel in distress that mindlessly waits for her prince kind of princess... but like Queen Elizabeth from the Crown or Princess Mia in Princess Diaries. They had to be trained on how to rule, lead a dignified life, and be strong even during the storms.

The whole chapter of Psalm 45 gives a beautiful glimpse into what it means to be noble but let's take this segment:

"Daughters of kings are among your honored women; at your right hand is the royal bride in gold of Ophir. Listen, daughter, and pay careful attention: Forget your people and your father's house. Let the king be enthralled by your beauty; honor him, for he is your lord."

–Psalm 45:9-11

How beautiful! In this small bit of scripture, 3 identities are called out of us: Daughter, Princess, Beautiful. Three of God's identities are also mentioned: King, Father, Lord. This chapter of Psalm was written for a specific family of nobility, but David sometimes carries a bit of prophecy through his poems, and I believe the deeper root of his intentions behind this chapter is our life of nobility under God as our King and Father.

What princess, fictional or not, do you admire and why?

The way God sees a father's heart is best reflected in the parable of the Prodigal son Jesus tells in Luke 15. This story has a lot of meaning that entire books could be written about, but the parts that are best for this chapter are in verses 12 and 20. This dignified, rich father had 2 sons. One of whom was ridiculously rude and demanded his inheritance even before his father died. This is like saying "I'm tired of waiting for you to die, just give me your money, which I don't deserve, right now! And I'll be on my merry way..." In verse 12, the father gives the rebellious son his money anyways. Rest assured he was probably dismayed at his son's actions, but this shows how the father is in tune to the heart of the son. He sees it's a hard decision to make and that the best course of action is to give him what he wants and encounter life on his own. The son soon learns that spending all your money on reckless living and prostitutes isn't the way to go and is so poor that he's left eating pig's slop! He decides to make a humble return home and ask to be a servant in his father's household. We then come to verse 20: While the son is still a long way off before he's even begged for forgiveness, the father picks up his robes and RUNS to his son! He proclaims to the servants, "Bring jewelry and clothes and food and throw a party! Celebrate my son's return!" Of course, the father in this story represents God the father and His character is revealed in this parable.

Humility and repentance are required on our part, but before we even get on our knees, He's eagerly running toward us to welcome us back home! Not only does this sound like the kind of King I'd like to serve, but he also sounds like a pretty sweet Dad.

What stirs in your heart when thinking of God as a Father?

The job of the King is to rule. To lead his Kingdom. The Kingdom of God is the most mysterious and complicated monarchy we can ever imagine. He is a patient king, a good king, a kind king, a just king and a wise king. And He has decided to delegate part of that responsibility to us as His trusted sons and daughters. For some reason, even though He could defeat Satan and end all wars with a snap of His fingers, He decided to choose us to fulfil His will. He decided to bring His children on His mission with Him. He decided to delegate the good works of the world to us, messy humans. He so graciously allowed us to be a part of the greatest love story ever told. He doesn't need to use us, but He wants to.

"Then God said, " Let us make mankind in our image, in our likeness, so that they may rule over the fish in the sea and the birds in the sky, over the livestock and all the wild animals, and overall the creatures that move along the ground." God blessed them and said to them, "Be fruitful and increase in number; fill the earth and subdue it. Rule over the fish in the sea and the birds in the sky and over every living creature that moves on the ground."

- Genesis 1:26, 28

God has chosen His ambassadors, His right hand, the beings in charge of reporting back to Him. God's intent is to entrust us, humans, with a mission to steward His creation and to do that alongside Him.

What is the first thing that comes into your mind when you think about authority?

There is something about our culture that has a hard time understanding authority. The Bible has a lot to say about it, but it's easy to brush it aside because of the confusion we experience nowadays. Authority is often confused with a sense of *dictatorship*. Because we live in a fallen world and have become messy, sinful people, it is inevitable that the people in authority will mess up, and this has given us a bad sense of authority altogether. Over the years, we have learned to fear authority because the people in authority are responsible for the decisions that affect the majority of people. Since our world is fallen and our nature is sinful, human authority often messes up. But in this chapter, I won't be talking a ton about the authority of man but rather of God.

How do you feel about God being your authority?

In contrast to our fallen, sinful, earthly authorities, God's authority is perfect. It's hard to imagine because we have no worldly examples of what it is like to be perfect or follow someone who is perfect. Did you know He can't mess up? Did you know He is incapable of sin? Did you know that His overflowing, overpowering love for us has caused Him to make the most radical of sacrifices just for us? His ruling is divine and true and right. Do you truly believe the creator of the universe is the epitome of perfection? Let's push all our hesitations about submission to authority aside because God is a good leader, unlike some abusive human authorities you might be thinking of right now. So, it's a blessing to follow Him. Think back to the prodigal son story... that portrays the heart of the father and leader we follow.

Now, there is something that God chose to do in the Genesis verse above, and that is, He decided to delegate. There are 2 clear missions that apply to mankind and believers as a whole. One is above where it says, "Be fruitful and multiply...rule" The other is in Matthew 28, when Jesus tells us, "Go and make disciples."

"And Jesus came and said to them, "All authority in heaven and on earth has been given to me. Go therefore and make disciples of all nations, baptizing them in[b] the name of the Father and of the Son and of the Holy Spirit, teaching them to observe all that I have commanded you. And behold, I am with you always, to the end of the age."

- Matthew 28:18-20

Rewrite this verse in your own words.

The King, who has no limitations, submitted his will to limited beings, both to multiply and make disciples. Our limited minds can't comprehend an unlimited being. What does it mean to not be bound by space or time? What could it possibly be like to speak things into existence? How could a being, no matter how divine, be impossibly and perfectly *good and just and loving?*

One of the greatest mysteries of this phenomenon is that he has decided to call us sons and daughters. Not just ambassadors but His most trusted and beloved family!

"I will be a father to you, and you shall be sons and daughters to me, says the Lord Almighty."

-2 Corinthians 6:18

"Yet to all who did receive him, to those who believed in his name, he gave the right to become children of God— children born not of natural descent, nor of human decision or a husband's will, but born of God."

-John 1:12-13

A new identity has been offered to us, and like all identities, all we need to do is accept it and it will have a drastic ripple effect on every action through the rest of our lives. He has given you the right and the gift to be His daughter. Are you going to believe it? Are you going to act like it?

To be honest, this is *such* a hard truth for me to accept. I remember when I was about 8, crying when I found out that God was my Dad. I loved my earthly Dad so much that I was grieved to think I actually had another Father! That's really an amazing testament to my Dad that he represented God's father heart so much that I didn't want any other father. However, he isn't perfect, and I must constantly remind myself that as amazing as my Dad is, it's only a glimpse of God's perfect parenting. How much more loving, powerful and thoughtful God must be if He's better than my Dad!

I also know some people who don't like accepting this identity of "daughter" because of the opposite reason! Their earthly dad was a poor representation of God's father heart, and so they don't see the value in having a father. But did you know that we have something inside of us that yearns for a father, a dad? We all know deep down that one of our core longings is for an Abba (Hebrew for Dad.)

"For you did not receive the spirit of slavery to fall back into fear, but you have received the Spirit of adoption as sons, by whom we cry, "Abba! Father!"

– Romans 8:15

Direct that desire to the Lord above! Daughter, I'm so sorry that you had a poor representation of God's love for you but be comforted! His love and Daddy spirit is perfect, pure and righteous. You will never be let down by Him.

Now that we have settled that God has a perfect and ultimate authority that He carries out with love and He has chosen to delegate some of that authority to humans... but not just delegate as ambassadors to call us His very own *children*. He wants His kids fighting by His side. With that understanding, we'll discuss how we can fulfill these missions with strength and dignity.

Recap this section in your own words. How can the God Truth of "God is our Father" help us have strength and dignity?

Application

Now that we've read into our role and mission as a daughter of the King, how can we apply this belief to the characteristics of Strength and Dignity?

You might be able to guess that this is my favorite chapter because it's also the one I decided to name the book after! But why, you may ask? As I was writing this book, I realized that all of these chapters and characteristics; wise, God-fearing, valuable, worthy, driven, enterprising, diligent, forward-thinking, fearless, generous, homemaker, respected and noble... they all have one thing in common. First, a lot of them are things we change inwardly. People might not see us being fearless or driven or valuable or noble. They might see us be enterprising or generous, but *how* are we to be enterprising or generous? How are we living any of these characteristics?

If we decide we are going to be driven but we do it in a way that pushes others down, and we only look out for ourselves, or if we decide to be fearless, but we instead act with recklessness... it's kind of beside the point, right? So, what I like so much about the words "strength and dignity" are that they show you *how* to portray the rest of these characteristics. Are you generous with a proud spirit? Or do you do it with humble dignity? Do you believe you are valuable with a desperate anxiety? Or with a solid strength? Are you forward-thinking with stress, fear, and distrust? Or do you laugh at the days to come with a resolute dignity?

But how do we get there? To the point where everything we do is done with strength and dignity? Let's chat about it.

. . . .

"Likewise also that women should adorn themselves in respectable apparel, with modesty and self-control, not with braided hair and gold or pearls or costly attire, but with what is proper for women who profess godliness—with good works."

- 1 Timothy 2:9-10

"Do not let your adorning be external—the braiding of hair and the putting on of gold jewelry, or the clothing you wear, but let your adorning be the hidden person of the heart with the imperishable beauty of a gentle and quiet spirit, which in God's sight is very precious."

-1 Peter 3:3-4

So, before you get mad at me for slipping these verses in here, first, I'll advise you to remember that these verses are in the Bible, and while they might not be our favorite, they are part of the Word we claim to follow. And second, all verses like these need a bit of cultural perspective. I won't dive into depth on the whole "no braids or jewelry" thing because this is more of a heart issue that Paul is addressing. In that era, women who adorned themselves like that when going to a church gathering were seen as prideful and arrogant and would draw attention to themselves when the real attention should be on God. So, I think it's safe to say that the real issue Paul wants us to stay away from is pride, but specifically *vanity*.

List 3 things from these verses that stuck out to you. Either that you have never heard before or you realize carry a weight to them.

I chose these verses because I think they list a few things God looks for or what He might see as dignified. Since Paul urges the women to not present themselves with pride, humility can be assumed to be a dignified trait. Being modest is one, and not simply modest in the way you dress! Modest really means you don't "flaunt" what you have, which could be your body. It could also be your talents or your status or your opportunity! Boasting or flaunting of any kind should always point back to Jesus, the one who is really deserving of praise. It also mentions the honorable traits of being respectable, self-controlled, doing good works, and having a gentle and quiet spirit... and it says these are *precious* to the Lord. I love that word. Our Father looks down at His daughters and calls us *precious* in His sight, and it's out of that love and acceptance that we are able to live with dignity.

"See what kind of love the Father has given to us, that we should be called children of God; and so we are. The reason why the world does not know us is that it did not know him."

-1 John 3:1

Rewrite this verse.

Darling, you are precious. You are fully known and fully loved. We can work our entire lives to be fully known and fully loved by people or one person, and our biggest fear is that someone will fully know us and not love us. But sit in this truth: He sees your faults, he sees your secrets, and he sees your sins and yet, He loves relentlessly. As you seek to deepen your relationship with and identity in Him, rest in the belief that you are held in His embrace.

As we are humbled by the idea that the mighty King that we just finished talking about in the section above has chosen to love us as daughters wholly and completely, how can dignity spill out of that? We have nothing to prove to the world. The one who created it already loves you! We can take our pride in being the daughter of the King, and not in the works we thought defined us.

. . . .

"But far be it from me to boast except in the cross of our Lord Jesus Christ, by which the world has been crucified to me, and I to the world."

-Galatians 6:14

Rewrite this verse.

You might have had someone in your life, maybe at school or work, who was just extremely hard to love and have grace for. They walked around with a chip on their shoulder, asking for attention or a fight. They so clearly had something to prove to the world in order to gain acceptance. Or maybe this person was/is you! It's not a very dignified way to live… don't you see why you don't have to be like that? You have freedom inside of the acceptance you have already gained with the Father! Freedom to be a solid dignified presence amidst a giant storm.

Write: I have freedom inside of the acceptance I have already gained with the Father.

This is a steady balance that takes time to find and can only be maintained through Christ. But once that balance is found, it becomes a force to be reckoned with, a rock for others to lean on, a center of gravity others can't help but admire and say, "Wow. What does she have? I want that." Invoke others to jealousy through your dignity so you can tell them, "I am only like this because of Jesus."

Journal about any actions, steps, thoughts or emotions this invokes in you.

But what about strength? Well, this brings us full circle to the idea that God is our King with authority that He has delegated to His children. This means we have to do something that might not sound very appealing.... We need to submit.

I KNOW, ew! That word isn't seen positively in these times. But to submit means to put yourself under the authority of someone else, and we are, right?

Have you had bad experiences submitting to authority? Talk about the aspects of this experience that are purely because of human's fallen state.

Nowadays, people don't like to value submission because they attribute it to weakness. It's a power play, and all people see is that leaders have power, and followers have less power, which is a negative thing. To that, I say: NO. Only the strongest people are able to submit. Do you know the amount of strength it takes to lift up your hands to the Lord and say, "Not my will but yours be done"? That feeling of putting everything you have into someone else's hands... It might feel vulnerable, but you must be strong to be vulnerable. Just like it takes strength to push down that bubble in your throat when you're about to open your innermost being to someone... it takes strength to admit you are not an all-knowing, all-powerful, all-consuming deity, and submit yourself to someone who is.

Journal about any actions steps, thoughts or emotions this invokes in you. Is there anything your godly authority might be wanting you to do that scares you?

Submission to our Lord requires strength and it must be carried out with a dignity that is precious in the sight of the Lord. We must fill the earth and subdue it with dignity, we must rule the earth with dignity, we must go and make disciples with dignity, and act on any other callings from God with dignity. And we must be strong to do so.

Group Questions

1. What does the identity as a Daughter of the King stir up in your heart?

2. What areas in your life are hard to submit to God?

3. In your own words, describe why it's important for us to have strength and dignity in all that we do.

4. List some practical ways your life or other characteristics might look if you lived them with strength and dignity.

Group Blessing

You are Lord of Lords and King of Kings. You are the strongest and dignified of all beings, and you call us to be just as you are. Instruct us in your ways. Ignite in us a strength that can only come from you. Bestow upon us a dignity that comes from an identity as a daughter of the King. When we stumble upon failure as we inevitably will, redeem us with your light and blood. Lift us up on your shoulders and train us yet again in your ways that we may never forget.

Amen.

Final Commission

Well ladies, you have come to the end! First, thank you for taking the time and energy to go through this book. My hopes for you after having gone through all this content is that you will have a fuller understanding of who God is and His perfect nature. May you find your value, worth and nobility in Him and believe at a 10 that He calls you into those identities. May your character become a force to be reckoned with. May you be a soldier of the Kingdom of God that makes the enemy tremble. May you steadfastly seek after the Lord's will, be continuously filled with the Holy Spirit, and become more like Jesus all the days of your life. May a spirit fill and surround you that makes everyone who encounters you stop and wonder what makes you different, and may you tell them about your source, the King. May you be filled with boldness to share the Gospel with those around you. And finally, may you clothe yourself with Strength & Dignity and laugh without fear of the future.

Authors

While his book was initiated by me (Kelsey), it was only through the hard work, wisdom, friendship, love, support and writing of these dear friends and family members that this book was made possible. I knew what type of book I wanted to exist, and I knew I could contribute a little to its contents, but I would need the combined wisdom and life experience of multiple women to make this a credible and worthwhile Bible Study. Please, read about these amazing women without whom this book wouldn't have been possible.

@addieparris

Addie first began following Christ after her freshman year of high school when she heard the Gospel in a way she could understand, especially when a mentor stepped in and showed her what a life with Jesus could look like. After striving for perfection and to just be "good enough," God began to show her how she didn't have to perform for approval and how she could rest in His love and grace. Addie's time in High School was where she really began to know and walk with Jesus, but it wasn't always easy. As someone who knows what it's like to follow Jesus in the teenage years, she's passionate about helping girls in the same position she was in before she followed Jesus, which is why she wanted to contribute to this book!

Addie is a recent college graduate from Northern Kentucky University and is a Young Life leader at a local high school. In her free time, she loves reading good books, traveling, and attempting to cook.

 jeffandalyssa.com

 @alyssajoybethke

Alyssa Bethke talks about marriage, family, real life, and how Jesus transforms it all and is our great hope. Alongside her husband, Jefferson Bethke, on YouTube videos and iTunes podcasts that are watched by hundreds of thousands of viewers each month. She loves being a mom to her three fun-loving kids Kinsley, Kannon and Lucy. She lives in Maui with her family and loves reading, painting, and laughing with her closest people.

 stasiarose.com

 @anastasiarjd

 hello@stasiarose.com

Anastasia is a blog coach, storyteller, and world traveler. She is the proud owner of www.stasiarose.com, a lifestyle blog dedicated to helping women find their voice and use their stories to change the world. Author of the book **Blog Like A Boss** *(the beginner's guide to next-level blogging on any platform)*, Anastasia is passionate about helping others leave a legacy and launch unique blogs of their own with purpose and intention. You can find her cozied up in coffee shops, armed with a journal, pen and a fresh cup of coffee (hold the cream and sugar, please).

Ebook: *www.amazon.com/Blog-Like-Boss-beginners-next-level-ebook/dp/ B01JNYOJQ4*

 April Pryor

April is a mother of five and wife to Jeremy going on 22 years! She grew up on the outskirts of Columbus, Ohio, in a faithful household with her parents and three siblings. Through her years of singleness, college, travel, daughterhood, wifehood, motherhood and following Jesus, she has continuously learned to grow deeper in her relationship with the Lord as He has challenged her and blessed her faithfully.

She likes learning new languages like American Sign Language and Hebrew, going on dates with her husband and sewing. She owns and runs a sewing shop with her mother, Julie and daughters. She has started three businesses, raised her five children, and contributed towards various books and other enterprises of family members or friends.

Julienne Scofield Seely

Julie grew up in a close-knit family on a central Ohio farm in post–World War II America. Married while still in college, then moving around the country with her husband's jobs, she met and received Christ and has been blessed by the fifty-two-year journey with Him while mothering her four children.

Widowed after fifty years, eight months, and two days, she has experienced the loneliness and loss of saying a temporary farewell to her other half. She is currently on the journey of giving up her old life and looks to the Bible passage of Proverbs 31 for guidance in redirecting her new one.

What makes her heart glow is interacting with her four adult children and their spouses, her twenty-four grandchildren and four great-grandchildren. She looks forward with great joy to meeting the three grandchildren and two great-grandchildren who are already in Heaven.

She has published a pro-life novel, *Mother, May I?* (available on Amazon) and is now writing her second book. Her current ministries include teaching needlework skills at her family's sewing studio in Ft. Thomas, Kentucky, as well as entering her fiftieth year of Bible teaching in her local church. She was blessed to be asked to contribute to this timely study being prepared by one of her grand-daughters.

Kelsey Pryor

 withstrengthanddignity.com

 @kelseyjoypryor

@_withstrengthanddignity_

Kelsey has spent her 20 years living at home with her Christian family of two parents and four siblings, traveling the States, traveling to Israel, writing, crafting, sewing, learning Hebrew and studying the Bible as she has grown in her relationship with the Lord. She has been a part of her family's numerous entrepreneurial efforts, the most recent of which are Just Sew (www.justsewstudio.com) and Family Teams (familyteams.com).

Her passions include her many hobbies, discipleship, Jesus, her family, and the nation of Israel. You can find her at a coffee shop with friends, teaching sewing classes at her family's store, in her room, devising her next big plan, vision or idea, curled on the couch with a sibling, or teaching and attending various Bible studies and faith-based events.

Her passion for writing and compiling this Bible study came out of her distress at the current state of femininity in the world. Plagued by questions like "What does it mean to be a woman, where do I find my value, what is a righteous way to live, and what does God say about me?" led her to reach out to some of her closest friends, gifted writers and women of God to help her create this resource for young single women.

@naomi_ferrari

Naomi is a 20-year-old CrossFit coach and athlete, who is currently working in full-time missions with the organization *Youth With A Mission*. She uses her passion for sports and fitness to bring discipleship through this avenue with the hopes of impacting people's lives from training inside gyms to competing in the sport.

She was raised in a house with 4 brothers by her single mother in the Midwest of America, and thanks her brothers for her competitive drive.

"When I was asked to contribute to this book, I was STOKED. I know that God is raising me up as a messenger for my generation and I believe I carry a message of faith. Part of my testimony is I believed for a long time that because of my life, I was inadequate and unqualified for God to use in big ways. But when I heard the full gospel for the first time as a teenager and I read through the Bible for the first time, I broke down when I learned about the wondrous, Just, loving lord and Father God we have. When I locked onto the gospel message for the first time, I've not let go since. I've done nothing but run hard after God, believing in the story, I get to be a part of and believing in my purpose of bringing glory to the name of Jesus. I want the Lamb to see the reward of his suffering, whether it's in my messages, when I compete in CrossFit, when I coach Athletes or when I'm with my family. I want to see the name of Jesus lifted high in my generation."

Acknowledgements

I have so many people I'd like to thank, who contributed to making this book possible.

- The first, of course, are the authors who agreed to come alongside me to make this thing happen! I knew I needed women who are wise with other life experiences and different perspectives to contribute to these pages, and I couldn't have asked for anyone better! Mom, Grandma, Anastasia, Alyssa, Addie and Naomi... I couldn't have done this without you. Thanks for believing in my vision and putting in the time and effort to make it happen!

- A special thanks to Addie for meeting with me for countless hours to plan out, revise and write this book. You're such a source of godly wisdom and encouragement. You're a dedicated, loving, and kind friend who so graciously reflects the heart of Jesus. I seriously couldn't have done this without you.

- To my sister Sydney and the artists Anna and Amy, who helped create this gorgeous book cover!

- To the women who took time out of their days to proofread, comment and edit the earliest versions of this book: Alexa Handelsman, Madison Theil, Maggie Woolf, Addie Parris & Heather Treas. Your feedback is invaluable to me, and I'm so blessed to be loved and supported by you.

- To my Dad, who met with me hours at a time, listened to each chapter as I read them aloud and offered his advice, wisdom, and praise to ensure the theological accuracy and fullness of potential within this written work. Thank you for always believing in me!

- To my dear cousin, Dove. Your photography talent is an obvious blessing to this work, and it wouldn't be what it is today without you! Thank you for being my hype man, my encouragement, and my late-night coffee date.

- To Addie Parris, Alexa Handelsman, Annabelle Lightner, Priya Zwolinski, Sydney and Elisa Pryor, Naomi Fierro and Kayla Ferguson for being in the pictures! Thanks for taking time to glam up and be my gorgeous models.

- To Chelsea Crockett Hurst, how I wish we are able to live more life together! Your steadfast faith and inspiration to countless women around the globe is inspirational, and I'm so thankful you decided this book was worthy of your time and contribution. You were one of my earliest role models through your online work, and to be able to work on something together is a dream come true.

○ And last but certainly not least, the 49 people who donated to my Kickstarter. This book CERTAINLY would not have been possible without your generous donations: Addie Parris, Alexandra Dieckmann, Angelica Schmitter, Annabelle Lightner, April Pryor, Benjamin Widmer, Blake Smith, Brianna Cummins, Michelle Perry, Colin Roth, Daniel Field, Dave McMurray, Elijah Preston, Elisabeth Sowle, Elisabeth Williams, Grant Dawson, Hannah Rogers, Heidi Noland, Henry Czeerwonka, Iryna, Jackson Pryor, Janet Pryor, Jeremy Pryor, Jill Petipas, Jon Putnam, Julianne Thompson, Justin Wolfenberg, Kandace Sipples, Kristy Nicholas, Kyle Ball, Laina Putnam, Liat Nesher, Mackenzie Ryan, Madison Theil, Mallory Gaetjens, Mark Parrett, Megan Pender, Melissa May, Nate Sallee, Nick Derington, Priya Zwolinski, Rebecca Lucy, Rob Ramey, Robert Asseo, Stephen Mowry, Tim Schmoyer, Wendy Ramirez, Witni Sztanyo. I appreciate your contributions! God bless you!!

Citations

a) Season 2, Episode 15 of the Jordan B. Peterson podcast.

b) *The Holy Bible*. Biblica Inc., New International Version, 2011.

c) *Big Magic: Creative Living Beyond Fear*, Elizabeth Gilbert. Bloomsbury Publishing Plc, 2015.

d) *The Holy Bible*. Crossway, English Standard Version, 2012.